Published by Shiloh Kidz, an imprint of Barbour Publishing, Inc., 1810 Barbour Drive, Uhrichsville, Ohio 44683, www.shilohkidz.com

Our mission is to inspire the world with the life-changing message of the Bible.

ecpa Member of the
Evangelical Christian
Publishers Association

Printed in the United States of America.
06701 1019 SP

CHOOSE KINDNESS

3-MINUTE DEVOTIONAL INSPIRATION
FOR KIDS

JOANNE SIMMONS

SHILOH ! kidz

An Imprint of Barbour Publishing, Inc.

INTRODUCTION

Kids like you today have about a zillion opportunities to do amazing things! In fact, you might feel like you never have enough time to do all the cool things that interest you. But in the midst of your busy life, do you know what there is *always* time for? Kindness. Nothing in your schedule of activities and schoolwork should ever stop you from spreading kindness among others and most importantly sharing kindness with God because of His great kindness and love for you! Sometimes being kind to others might feel super hard, but everyone can make choices to love kindness, learn kindness, and live in kindness. Turn the page and read on for scriptures, prayers, and reflections to help you choose kindness every single day!

CREATOR OF KINDNESS

God is love.
1 JOHN 4:16

Dear God, these days it's most popular to just believe in science and not in You as Creator, but if it's true that people just eventually appeared because of some scientific explosion, then where do our kindness and love even come from? Nothing in our entire scientific world has love for each other like human beings do. And then You remind me that every single person is not just some random product of a big bang. You whisper to my heart and soul that You are the Creator of every person; we are all made in Your image. You are love itself, and all love comes from You. Kindness is part of Your love, and You want us to learn real love from You and share it with others. Teach me Your kindness, God. Fill me up to bubbling over with it. Let those bubbles of kindness touch every person I come in contact with, I pray. Amen.

In what ways are you letting God teach
you about His love and kindness?

THE GREATEST KINDNESS EVER!

But God showed His love to us.
While we were still sinners, Christ died for us.

ROMANS 5:8

Dear God, this verse briefly describes the greatest kindness the world has ever known—You sent Your one and only Son to take the punishment for every single person's sin. And then You ask us to just admit that we all sin and believe that You suffered and died to take our sin away from us. And You didn't stay dead. You rose again and defeated death, and You offer eternal life to all of us! We simply have to believe in You and ask You to be our Savior from sin. Then You will help us live our best lives for You as we seek You. Wow! You are the one true God and the kindest and most loving One *ever*! I trust You as my only hope and Savior, Jesus. Thank You! Amen.

....

Do you believe in Jesus as your Savior?

RETURNING GOD'S KINDNESS

*Whoever obeys His Word has the love of God made perfect
in him. This is the way to know if you belong to Christ.
The one who says he belongs to Christ should
live the same kind of life Christ lived.*

1 John 2:5–6

Dear God, You have been so kind to me by offering
me salvation from my sins and promising me life with
You forever. I can't ever thank You enough or share
enough kindness in return for that, but I do want to
try. I know the best way to share kindness with You
is to obey the teaching of Your Word, the Bible. That's
a win-win, for sure, because it pleases You and brings
glory to You, and it also blesses me with the best kind
of life possible—a life lived for You, like Jesus lived.
Please help me to obey You with all of my heart, all of
the time. Amen.

....

In what ways are you actively obeying God's Word?
How will you continue to grow in obedience to God?

MORE BUBBLES

Loving-favor and loving-kindness and peace are ours
as we live in truth and love. These come from God
the Father and from the Lord Jesus Christ,
Who is the Son of the Father.

2 JOHN 1:3

Dear God, I love the idea of kindness bubbling out of me. What a fun thought! Who doesn't love to blow bubbles sometimes? I've loved them ever since I was tiny, and they're not just for babies. I think everyone, grown-ups too, could use a little more relaxing bubble-blowing time in their lives! Bubbles are peaceful and end with a pop of delight. I want to share kindness that brings peace and delight to others too—peace and delight that ultimately come from You! Thank You! Amen.

How do you keep yourself filled up to bubbling over with God's love, kindness, and peace?

SHARING THE GREATEST KINDNESS EVER

*"You are to go to all the world and preach
the Good News to every person."*

MARK 16:15

Dear Jesus, I don't ever want to forget about how You came to earth as a baby, lived Your life to help others know God, died to save people from their sin, and then rose again to conquer death and offer eternal life to anyone who believes in You! That is the Good News, the awesome message of the Gospel, and I want to share it with others. It's the greatest kindness I can ever do—telling people about You! Help me to talk to others about You and Your great love all the time. Please give me many opportunities. Amen.

How can you make sharing about Jesus and the
Gospel a regular part of your conversations?

MATCHING UP

They say they know God, but by the way they act, they show
that they do not. They are sinful people. They will not
obey and are of no use for any good work.

Titus 1:16

Dear God, I've heard the saying "Actions speak louder than words," and I think it's so true. I want the things I say about You—that I love You and follow You and Your Word—to match up with what I'm actually doing. I know how frustrating it is to watch someone say nice things but act in terrible ways. That's called being a hypocrite, and I don't ever want to be that. I know I can't be perfect, but I want to do my best at saying I love and live for You and actually doing that. Please help me live out my faith in You in ways that make others want to follow You too. I'm so thankful You are leading me! Amen.

Are your words about God matching
up with your actions?

WHEN I DON'T FEEL LIKE BEING KIND

*Let us go with complete trust to the throne of God.
We will receive His loving-kindness and have His
loving-favor to help us whenever we need it.*

HEBREWS 4:16

Dear God, sometimes I don't feel like bubbling over with kindness one bit! There are all kinds of things that make me feel too mad or too sad or too frustrated or just too tired to share anything nice with anyone at all! When those times happen, could You please remind me how close You are to me? I want to remember You are always available to help. I don't want my upset feelings to make me act unkindly toward others. Please help me to choose kindness even when it's hard. Thank You! Amen.

. . . .

What are the things that sometimes make
you feel like acting out in unkind ways?

KINDLY OBEYING

Children, as Christians, obey your parents. This is the right thing to do. Respect your father and mother. This is the first Law given that had a promise. The promise is this: If you respect your father and mother, you will live a long time and your life will be full of many good things.

EPHESIANS 6:1–3

Dear God, I'm very thankful for my parents and how they love and take good care of me. Sometimes I don't show kindness well to them, though, because I disobey or disrespect them. Sometimes I don't even know why I treat them poorly; it just seems to happen. That is because of sin in me, and I need Your help to fight sin. Please forgive me for acting badly toward my parents. Please help me to be kind and to obey them and to apologize and make things right quickly when I do mess up. Amen.

In what ways do you find it hardest to obey and respect your parents? How can you improve in those areas?

SURPRISING MOM AND DAD

*"Honor your father and your mother, so your life may be
long in the land the Lord your God gives you."*

EXODUS 20:12

Dear God, please help me to think of fun ways to surprise my parents with kindness! I love when they spend time with me, and I realize they are busy with lots of responsibilities. Help me to think of ways I can lighten their loads by doing chores they didn't have to ask me to do or picking up after myself without reminders or helping take care of younger siblings. They do so much for me, and I want to return their generosity and kindness. Please fill me up with joy from doing helpful things for my parents. I love my parents and I am grateful to You for them, God. Please bless them through me. Amen.

· ·

What are some of the ways you know
your parents appreciate your help?

WHEN THINGS ARE TOUGH AT HOME

Give all your cares to the Lord and He will give you strength.
He will never let those who are right with Him be shaken.

PSALM 55:22

Dear God, when my parents are sick or maybe just really stressed out, please help me to show them extra, *extra* kindness and encouragement. Help us all to have tons of patience with each other in our family. Illness and anxiety can cause a lot of trouble in a family, but with Your help that doesn't need to happen. Help us to get closer to You when we experience problems. You give the peace and comfort and guidance and love that we need. You show us Your kindness and care in countless ways. Help me to show kindness and care as well in whatever ways You ask me to. Amen.

What causes stress at home, and how can you
show extra kindness during those times?

KINDNESS FOR OLDER FOLKS

Do not speak sharp words to an older man.
Talk with him as if he were a father.

1 TIMOTHY 5:1

Dear God, thank You for the grandparents, great-grandparents, and other older people in my life. Help me to show lots of kindness to them, especially using my energy that is probably a lot greater than theirs since my body is young! I want to help older people rather than wear them out. I want to learn from them because they usually have a lot of knowledge and wisdom. Help me to be kind to elderly people by showing extra respect for them, helping out with anything they need, and simply listening to them and learning from them. Amen.

....

Who are the elderly people in your life to whom you can show extra kindness?

EYES EVERYWHERE

The eyes of the Lord are in every place,
watching the bad and the good.

PROVERBS 15:3

Dear God, I love knowing that You are always watching me! I guess if some people have bad things to hide, they might not like this verse. But I don't ever want to hide from You. If I'm ever tempted to try to hide from You, please quickly remind me of Your great love for me. Help me to share with others how You love everyone so much that You are always looking out for us and taking care of us. You are always available to call on in prayer too! It's mind-boggling to think this is true for every person on earth—You care and see each and every one of us. You are amazing, God, and I praise You! Amen.

How are you comforted and strengthened
knowing that God is always watching you?

KINDNESS TOWARD SIBLINGS

Put out of your life all these things: bad feelings about other people, anger, temper, loud talk, bad talk which hurts other people, and bad feelings which hurt other people. You must be kind to each other. Think of the other person.

EPHESIANS 4:31–32

Dear God, it's so easy to fight with my siblings. They just annoy me so much sometimes! Or they mess with my stuff without asking. Or they just won't do what I want them to do! Help me to realize my fault in a lot of these fights I have with them. Help me to choose kindness toward them instead of the selfish reactions I often have when they're bugging me. Help me to talk things out and compromise with them in kind ways rather than fight. It might be hard, but I know You can guide me in this. Thank You! Amen.

What do you fight about most with your siblings? How can you work on showing kindness to them?

SIBLING ENCOURAGEMENT

Say what is good. Your words should help
others grow as Christians.

EPHESIANS 4:29

Dear God, when things are going great with my siblings, please help me remember to thank them for good relationships. I want to appreciate those times when we're getting along well! When we notice and celebrate the good times, we'll want them to continue in the future. When we encourage each other with the positive, we help each other avoid the negative. Our relationships will never be perfect, but with Your help we can choose kindness toward each other so much more than we choose meanness toward each other. When we do mess up, please help us to apologize, communicate and learn from each other well, and forgive ASAP! Amen.

What are your favorite times with your siblings?
How can you continue to make great
memories with them?

KINDLY FORGIVING

You must be kind to each other. Think of the other person.
Forgive other people just as God forgave you
because of Christ's death on the cross.

EPHESIANS 4:32

Dear God, thank You for Your kindness to me in that You forgive me again and again and again, sometimes for the same kind of thing I keep doing wrong over and over. I get so frustrated with myself for my mistakes, and I'm so grateful that Your grace is endless. That means You don't hold my mistakes against me. Your Word says You take my sins away from me "as far as the east is from the west" (Psalm 103:12). Wow! I don't know what I would ever do without Your love and grace, God. Your forgiveness is incredibly kind, and I want to model it and try to be as forgiving to others as You are to me. Please help me! Amen.

What has God forgiven you of? How do you offer that same kind of forgiveness to others?

BEING KIND TO YOURSELF

Nothing should be done because of pride or thinking about yourself. Think of other people as more important than yourself. Do not always be thinking about your own plans only. Be happy to know what other people are doing.

PHILIPPIANS 2:3–4

Dear God, the world talks a lot about focusing on *myself* and being *my* best and following *my* dreams and doing what feels right for *me* rather than others. But Your Word says to humble myself and look out for others. I want to do what *You* want, God, not what this world tells me. Help me to figure this out well. It's obvious I do have to take good care of myself and do my best to stay healthy to be able to serve others and do the good things You have planned for me. But I want to do that in wise and unselfish ways that please You while showing constant kindness and care toward others as well. Thank You for helping me with this! Amen.

....

What are ways you take care of yourself unselfishly that allow you to care well for others?

THE BEST KINDNESS TO YOURSELF

Come close to God and He will come close to you.

JAMES 4:8

Dear God, I think the very best way I can be kind to myself is by spending lots of time with You! Help me to make my relationship with You my top priority in life. There are so many things I let get in the way of spending time with You, and I'm sorry. Please forgive me. Please fill me with joy in spending time reading Your Word, praying to You, worshipping You, going to church to learn more about You, and serving You. Make me want more and more and even more time with You! I want to be hooked on my time with You above anything else! Amen.

....

When and where and how often do you spend time with God? How can you spend even more focused time with Him?

HEALTHY HABITS

God bought you with a great price. So honor God with your body. You belong to Him.

1 CORINTHIANS 6:20

Dear God, making good choices can be hard when it comes to healthy eating and exercise habits. So much tasty junk food is available these days! I have a lot of favorite foods that really aren't very good for me. Can You help me develop healthy habits? I need wisdom to make good food choices, like grabbing an apple or carrots for a snack rather than potato chips or candy. I also need to make sure I don't lie around being lazy too much. My body needs to move around—playing sports and games and dancing and running and doing all kinds of fun physical activity. Please help me be kind to my body by getting the exercise it needs. I want to have healthy habits that honor You, God! Thank You for creating me! Amen.

What are your healthy habits? What are some unhealthy ones you could change?

WISDOM WITH SOCIAL MEDIA

*So be careful how you live. Live as men who are wise
and not foolish. Make the best use of your time.*
EPHESIANS 5:15–16

Dear God, social media is such a big deal these days.
Can You please help me not to get too caught up in
it? I want to be kind to myself and not worry about it
too much. Some people I know seem to spend all their
time using it and obsessing over it, and that doesn't
seem like a good idea. Please help me to have good
friendships and social time without phones or the in-
ternet involved. And please guide me in knowing how
and when to use social media in wise ways. Amen.

....

How often do you use social media?
What are some good things about it,
and what are some bad things about it?

MORE WISDOM WITH SOCIAL MEDIA

Whatever you say or do, do it in the name of the Lord Jesus.
Give thanks to God the Father through the Lord Jesus.

COLOSSIANS 3:17

Dear God, I hear a lot about people being mean and arguing in nasty ways on social media. If or when I do use it, I never want to be a part of that. I only want to use it in positive ways that please You and encourage others. The world has enough mean stuff going on; we sure don't need to spread around meanness or negativity on social media! Help me to use social media as a tool for encouragement and kindness. Amen.

Have you seen people being mean on social media?
What are specific ways people can use it to
spread kindness and encouragement?

WITH A SMILE AT SCHOOL

Whatever work you do, do it with all your heart. Do it for the Lord and not for men. Remember that you will get your reward from the Lord. He will give you what you should receive. You are working for the Lord Christ.

COLOSSIANS 3:23–24

Dear God, there are things I love about school and things that drive me crazy about it. Can You please help me keep a good attitude about school no matter what is going on there? I want to show kindness to teachers and staff by being respectful and easygoing and listening and following rules (even if I think some of the rules are silly). Help me to focus on what I'm at school for—good learning—rather than the frustrating and annoying things that sometimes happen. Please help me to do my best work with a smile at school, all to give You praise! Amen.

....

What do you love about school? What drives you crazy? How does God help in all of these things?

DURING DIFFICULT SCHOOL DAYS

Open your heart to teaching, and your ears
to words of much learning.

PROVERBS 23:12

Dear God, there is a particular teacher at school who is just so hard to learn from. I don't enjoy the class at all, and the rules and homework and requirements seem over-the-top ridiculous! I don't want to just whine about it, but it's all so frustrating! Please give me wisdom to know how to control my feelings of frustration and to choose kindness and respect for my teacher during this class. Please help me to be able to communicate well and handle the workload, and also help me not to join in saying unkind things along with other students. Please work out this tough situation. I know You care about everything going on in my life, God. Thank You! Amen.

....

What has been your toughest situation with
a teacher at school? How did God help?

KINDNESS TO ENEMIES

"I say to you who hear Me, love those who work against you.
Do good to those who hate you. Respect and give thanks for
those who try to bring bad to you. Pray for those
who make it very hard for you."

LUKE 6:27–28

Dear God, I know some truly mean kids. The way they treat others is awful. They've been nasty to me and to some of my friends. They sure seem like enemies. I want to be mean back, but I know You've said I should love and pray for my enemies. Showing kindness to them is really hard. Please guide me in Your will in this, God. I sure can't do it on my own. Help me to see positive changes in these kids as I pray for them and act kindly toward them. Thank You! Amen.

....

Even if an enemy doesn't change as you pray,
how does praying for them change you?

FINDING GOOD FRIENDS

Do not let anyone fool you. Bad people can make
those who want to live good become bad.

1 CORINTHIANS 15:33

Dear God, I know I should show kindness to everyone, but that doesn't mean I have to be close friends with everyone. Your Word tells me I should be careful to choose good friends to hang out with. Help me be kind to myself by looking for friends who will have a good influence on me, not a bad one. Please give me good friendships with other kids who love You and who encourage me to get closer to You. Guide me to the close friends you want me to have, God, while also helping me show kindness to everyone around me, even those I'll never become BFFs with. Amen.

....

Who are your very best friends and why?

EVEN WHEN I'M SICK

A glad heart is good medicine.
PROVERBS 17:22

Dear God, it stinks to get sick or injured, and it's hard to be kind when I don't feel good. Please help me focus on all that I have to be grateful for when I'm sick. Thank You for my parents and all of the people You have put in my life who help take care of me. Thank You for doctors and nurses who care and for medicine that helps me get better, even if it tastes disgusting! Help me to focus on gratitude even when I'm sick. Then please help me turn that gratitude into kindness by saying thanks to those who care for me and by doing my best to keep a good attitude through illness and injury. Amen.

....

What's the worst illness or injury you've had? How did God help you through it in big ways and little ways?

WHEN I'M NOT SURE HOW TO HELP

The Holy Spirit helps us where we are weak. We do not know how to pray or what we should pray for, but the Holy Spirit prays to God for us with sounds that cannot be put into words.

ROMANS 8:26

Dear God, sometimes I just don't know how to show kindness to someone who has a lot of needs. Help me to remember that I can always pray to You for other people's needs. Telling You their names and needs and asking for You to do things I can't for them is always a kind choice. Please bring others into their lives who can help too. When I don't know what to pray, Your Word promises that Your Holy Spirit does the talking for me. Thank You for caring about everyone's needs no matter how big or small, God! Amen.

What was a time you didn't know how to help someone, but you prayed and God provided in a totally unexpected way?

HELP FROM THE HELPER

"The Helper is the Holy Spirit. The Father will send Him in My place. He will teach you everything and help you remember everything I have told you."

JOHN 14:26

Dear God, I need Your wisdom to know how best to share kindness with others. Please help me to know who needs it from me most and when. I still have so much learning to do! Thank You that You have given Your Holy Spirit to teach me everything. I'm so glad You are so near to me. I want to be a good listener and always keep learning from You, no matter how old I get. Amen.

. . . .

Do you feel like you are a good listener to God?
How can you always keep getting
better at listening to Him?

PRAYING FOR FRUIT

The fruit that comes from having the Holy Spirit in our lives is:
love, joy, peace, not giving up, being kind, being good, having
faith, being gentle, and being the boss over our own desires.

GALATIANS 5:22–23

Dear God, I love to eat fruit, but Your Word talks about another kind of good fruit—the fruit of the Spirit! Please grow it in me so much it's like huge baskets inside of me are overflowing with beautiful fresh pieces of it! If I have lots of it, I will have plenty to give to others, including loads of kindness! Thank You that Your Holy Spirit can do this kind of work in my life! Amen.

Have you memorized the fruit of the Spirit scripture
(Galatians 5:22–23)? If not, do so now and think
about it daily and ask God to constantly
grow this fruit in You!

WHEN I NEED SOME SPACE

Try to understand other people. Forgive each other. If you have
something against someone, forgive him. That is the way the
Lord forgave you. And to all these things, you must add love.
Love holds everything and everybody together
and makes all these good things perfect.

COLOSSIANS 3:13–14

Dear God, my little brother constantly wants to do what I'm doing. I feel like he never leaves me alone! I just need some space. But I know I shouldn't be mean to him. Please help me to be kind. Please remind me that he looks up to me. I need You, God, to guide me in how to communicate well that I love him and I love spending time with him, but sometimes I also need time to myself. You love us both, heavenly Father, and I know You want us to have a good relationship. Thank You for my brother. Amen.

....

What kinds of things do you love
doing with a younger sibling?

PATIENT KINDNESS

God has chosen you. You are holy and loved by Him. Because of this, your new life should be full of loving-pity. You should be kind to others and have no pride. Be gentle and be willing to wait for others.

COLOSSIANS 3:12

Dear God, I have trouble being patient sometimes. I don't like to wait. It's boring and frustrating! But when I stop to think about it, being patient is such a simple way to share kindness. It doesn't help anyone, including myself, to whine and complain when I have to wait on something or someone. Please help me to think of good things to do while I'm feeling impatient with waiting. Remind me I can always talk to You in my mind no matter where I am or what I'm doing! That is *always* a wonderful thing!

In what situations do you find it hardest to be patient? How can you work on becoming a more patient person?

BE A HELPER

*"In every way I showed you that by working hard like this we
can help those who are weak. We must remember what the
Lord Jesus said, 'We are more happy when
we give than when we receive.'"*

ACTS 20:35

Dear God, I know kids and adults with special needs,
and I want to show extra kindness to them! I'm amazed
and inspired by how they work through their challenges.
Help me to be a helper to them and their families. You
know all the details of their specific needs, and You can
help me encourage and bless them in specific ways. I
want to be filled with joy from serving and caring for
others that way. Thank You for loving every single
person so well, God! Amen.

....

How has a person with special needs been a blessing to
you? How can you bless them in return?

FOOD ALLERGIES

Help each other in troubles and problems.
This is the kind of law Christ asks us to obey.

GALATIANS 6:2

Dear God, a lot of kids have food allergies these days. At school and during other activities, help me be careful not to have foods around them that aren't good or safe for them. Sometimes I see other kids not caring or teasing them about their food allergies; they can be so mean! Even if they don't understand it, they can be thankful they don't struggle with food allergies and be kind and respectful to others who do. Help me to be a person who wants to show concern and understanding. Amen.

....

Do you—or maybe a friend or a loved one—have a
food allergy? What are some ways you or
they appreciate kindness because of it?

SICKNESS AND SCHOOLWORK

Dear friend, I pray that you are doing well in every way.
I pray that your body is strong and well even as your soul is.

3 JOHN 2

Dear God, one of the hardest parts of getting sick is missing school and then having makeup work to do. When I'm the one who has been sick, I sure appreciate when teachers and classmates are kind to me and patient with me by helping me through that makeup work. Please remind me to be a helpful friend to my classmates after they have been sick. I want to offer my help to get them caught up, because I know it's a great way to show kindness that is really appreciated. Amen.

•••

Have you ever been sick and missed a lot of school?
Who helped you and how?

ALL PEOPLE EVERYWHERE

*The Lord is not slow about keeping His promise as some people
think. He is waiting for you. The Lord does not want any person
to be punished forever. He wants all people to be sorry
for their sins and turn from them.*

2 PETER 3:9

Dear God, help me to remember that every single person
I meet or encounter or become friends with is created by
You and loved by You, and You want to save them from
sin. I can't do something kind for everyone I cross paths
with, but I *can* remember that You love all people and
I *can* pray for any person, anywhere. I can be willing to
serve and obey You in whatever ways You ask me to share
kindness in the little and the big moments of my days. I
trust that You want every single person on earth to turn
away from sin and believe in You as Savior. Help me to
do whatever kind things I can to help people understand
and accept Your truth and love. Amen.

....

Have you ever felt God asking you
to pray for a complete stranger?

SADNESS AND WORRIES

Give all your worries to Him because He cares for you.

1 PETER 5:7

Dear God, I know sometimes people don't like to share that they are feeling sad or worried. Help me to sense those feelings in others around me. Help me to be someone who notices and cares, even if that just means I pray silently for them. But help me to know when to be bold and reach out to them too, so they know that I care and can pray for them. Sometimes I feel sad and I'm not sure how to share my feelings with others either. I'm so glad we can always express our hearts to You, God! You are so kind to care about our sadness and worries, and I want to share Your kindness. Amen.

....

How does God comfort and calm you when you're sad or worried? How can you share that with others?

IN SPORTS AND ACTIVITIES

Make each other strong as you are already doing. We ask you,
Christian brothers, to respect those who work among you.
The Lord has placed them over you and they are your teachers.
You must think much of them and love them because
of their work. Live in peace with each other.

1 THESSALONIANS 5:11–13

Dear God, I want to show kindness in the sports, activities, and hobbies I'm involved in. Please help me to be a good teammate. Help me to be a good sport in both winning and losing. Please help me to be coachable and teachable. Help me to be friendly, kind, and encouraging to kids involved in the same activities and hobbies with me. I want to build up other kids around me and never tear them down. Thank You for all the cool opportunities I have! Amen.

....

What are your favorite sports and activities? What are the specific ways you show kindness during them?

DURING DISCOURAGEMENT

Comfort those who feel they cannot keep going on. Help the weak. Understand and be willing to wait for all men.

1 Thessalonians 5:14

Dear God, sometimes I get discouraged when things aren't going well for me. Maybe it's when I'm struggling with extra-hard homework or when a family problem at home doesn't ever seem to work out well. I definitely need extra kindness from You and from others during those times, and I'm so thankful You give it. Please help me to be someone who gives kindness to others when I can tell they are discouraged. Use me constantly to encourage others. It's a huge blessing to them and to me—and to You! You love to see people helping each other. Amen.

. . . .

Have you ever been super discouraged? What helped?
How does that motivate you to encourage others?

DOING WHAT GOD WANTS

Be full of joy all the time. Never stop praying. In everything give thanks. This is what God wants you to do because of Christ Jesus.

1 THESSALONIANS 5:16–18

Dear God, I love this scripture because sometimes I wonder what You want me to do, and this says it so simply. You want me to be full of joy all the time. You want me to never stop talking to You in prayer. And You want me to keep giving thanks in everything. I can do all those things! And when I do, I show great kindness to You, to myself, and to others. Even when awful things are going on around me, I can choose to have a joy that is based on You, not circumstances. I can constantly ask for Your help and thank You for the things I have to be grateful for. When others see this example in me, I pray that they will join me in doing what You want us to do! Amen.

Is 1 Thessalonians 5:16–18 hard or easy for you to obey? How can you work on doing what God wants?

KINDNESS TO HOMELESS AND NEEDY

He who gives to the poor will never want, but many bad things
will happen to the man who shuts his eyes to the poor.

PROVERBS 28:27

Dear God, I feel sad thinking about what it must be like to be homeless or unable to buy food or clothes. Please help me to have compassion for poor and needy people. Help me to think about and pray for them. Please help my family and me to be generous and wise in knowing how to give and to help. We can always pray and donate items and work together with our church to provide for needy people in our community. Please help more and more people to join with us in choosing kindness to those in need. Amen.

Have you ever been worried you wouldn't have
your basic needs met, like a home, food,
and clothing? How did God provide?

BLESSING LEADERS AT SCHOOL

He who follows what is right and loving and kind finds life, right-standing with God and honor.

PROVERBS 21:21

Dear God, I'm sure it can't be easy to be a teacher or principal or staff person at my school. A lot goes on at school every day! Please give me ideas for ways to be an encouragement to teachers and staff at school. For sure, I should be on my best behavior and listening and learning well. That's the best way to help. Please also show me other ways to bless and encourage everyone who works so hard to give me and all the other students a good education. Amen.

....

How do you feel when you get into trouble at school? How do you feel when you do something helpful and kind for a teacher at school?

EQUALLY LOVED

"The Lord does not look at the things man looks at. A man looks at the outside of a person, but the Lord looks at the heart."

1 Samuel 16:7

Dear God, when I see someone being treated badly because of the way they look or their skin color, I get so angry. It's not fair at all! You made every person beautiful and unique, and we are all equally loved by You! I wish we would all be like You and look at the heart of a person, not their outer appearance. If I see anyone being mistreated for their looks, please help me to be strong and brave and stand up to the bullies. Help me to show extra kindness and love to the one being mistreated. Help me to know how and when to get grown-ups involved to stop the bullying. Amen.

....

Have you or a friend ever experienced bullying because of your appearance? How did that feel? How did God help?

SIMPLE KINDNESS

*Pleasing words are like honey. They are sweet to
the soul and healing to the bones.*

PROVERBS 16:24

Dear God, please remind me to do little things that
can give really big encouragement to others. Just simple notes with kind words stuck on desks or lockers
of my classmates can make someone's day. Or I can
have fun making cards to deliver to residents at local nursing homes. Or I can write letters to people in
the military thanking them for serving and protecting
our country. Too often I get focused on myself and my
busy schedule and forget to do nice little things like
this. Please help me remember. Amen.

Who are some friends or loved ones who could be
encouraged greatly right now by a simple
note of kind words from you?

KINDNESS THROUGH CHURCH

Let us help each other to love others and to do good.
Let us not stay away from church meetings.

HEBREWS 10:24–25

Dear God, I know I can show great kindness to others by helping out in my local church. When people in my community gather regularly to worship You and learn about You and serve You by volunteering at church and helping people in need, we shine Your light and share Your love with our community and world in such a big way! I can do my part by being eager to participate at church every week. I also can encourage my whole family to go to church and take part in opportunities to serve others! Please help me and my family to love and support our church as much as possible. Amen.

Where do you go to church,
and what do you love most about it?

KINDNESS TO CHURCH LEADERS

*Christ. . .gave others the gift to be church leaders and teachers.
These gifts help His people work well for Him. And then the
church which is the body of Christ will be made strong.*

EPHESIANS 4:11–12

Dear God, thank You for pastors, teachers, and leaders at church. They give their time and talent to teach me and to help me grow in my relationship with You. Please help me to think of good ideas for ways to bless them. It might be as simple as thank-you notes and encouraging cards, or maybe with my parents' help I can give them a gift of thanks. For sure, I can give them good behavior, listening ears, and a teachable attitude. I also can pray for them regularly. They show kindness in wanting to teach me and guide me toward You, and I want to be kind to them in return! Amen.

....

What leaders and teachers at church are you especially thankful for? Be sure to tell them you appreciate them!

SHARING WORSHIP

*Keep on teaching and helping each other. Sing the Songs
of David and the church songs and the songs of
heaven with hearts full of thanks to God.*

COLOSSIANS 3:16

Dear God, I love singing songs of worship to You! One simple way I can be kind to others is by sharing songs with them. That doesn't mean I have to sing a solo to everyone, but I can join in happily with the singing at church to have shared worship with others. I can tell about the song message and lyrics to others outside my church too. And if I do enjoy singing solos, I can sing a song out loud for family and friends to hear. Music with words that help us focus on You is the best kind of music! I want to bless others around me with it. Please fill me up with joy as I do it! Amen.

....

What are your favorite worship songs?

KINDNESS TO GRIEVING PEOPLE

The Lord is near to those who have a broken heart.

PSALM 34:18

Dear God, it's so hard and sad to lose a loved one. I have hurt so much over it, and I have friends and family who hurt from the pain of losing loved ones too. Please help us all. Thank You for the way You are extra close to people who are brokenhearted with grief. Thank You for the friends and family who gather to honor the person who died and to help the people who are grieving the loss. Grief takes a long time to diminish. Help me to show extra-special kindness to people who are grieving. Amen.

....

What helped you most when you were grieving?
What are specific ways you can show
kindness to grieving people?

GRATEFUL, NOT GREEDY

He who loves money will never have enough money to make
him happy. It is the same for the one who loves to
get many things. This also is for nothing.

ECCLESIASTES 5:10

Dear God, I really, really need Your help not to be greedy. There are so many cool things I'd like to have. Especially when I see things my friends have that I don't, I struggle with jealousy and greediness to have more than I already do. Help me to look around at what I have and be grateful. Help me to show kindness by being interested in what my friends have without thinking I need to have all the same things too. Please bless me in ways that You know are best for me, God. Amen.

What are the things that are hardest
for you not to be greedy for?

KINDNESS TO A WORRIED FRIEND

"Do not worry. Do not keep saying, 'What will we eat?' or,
'What will we drink?' or, 'What will we wear?' The people who
do not know God are looking for all these things. Your Father
in heaven knows you need all these things. First of all, look
for the holy nation of God. Be right with Him. All these other
things will be given to you also. Do not worry about tomorrow.
Tomorrow will have its own worries. The troubles
we have in a day are enough for one day."

MATTHEW 6:31–34

Dear God, I have a friend who is worried about his dad losing his job. Please help me to show him kindness and to encourage him with this scripture from Matthew 6. I know You will take care of every one of his and his family's needs. Thank You for being our loving provider! Amen.

Have your parents ever experienced the loss of a job?
How did that affect your family?

KINDNESS AT NURSING HOMES

My body and my heart may grow weak,
but God is the strength of my heart and all I need forever.
PSALM 73:26

Dear God, I know visiting elderly and special needs people in nursing homes is a kind thing to do. Most of them love visitors. Help me to want to make time for visiting and to ask my parents or other grown-ups to take me or join up with a church group that regularly visits nursing homes. Help me to know what kind and encouraging things to say to the residents there. I love what Psalm 73:26 says to encourage people whose bodies are growing weak. You are their strength and everything they need. God, You are also my strength and everything I need. Thank You! Amen.

Why do you think nursing home residents are so encouraged by visits from young people like you?

MORE KINDNESS AT NURSING HOMES

God has given each of you a gift. Use it to help each other.
1 PETER 4:10

Dear God, working at a nursing home must be a challenging and sometimes sad job. I'm guessing those workers need a lot of kindness and encouragement. When I visit, help me to remember to thank the caregivers for all the hard work they do. I could make cards for them and maybe even make homemade treats to share too. Please strengthen and bless the caregivers of elderly and special needs residents at nursing homes, and show me how to be a blessing to them. Amen.

What do you think are some of the hardest
things about working at a nursing home?
What might be the joys of working there?

MANNERS MATTER

*Do for other people what you would like
to have them do for you.*

LUKE 6:31

Dear God, help me to remember that one simple way to show kindness is by having good manners everywhere I go. I want to show grown-ups I have polite behavior—in stores, at restaurants, when visiting relatives and friends, no matter where I am! Help me to listen well, speak kindly, hold doors for others, let others go first. . .all those little things that really do mean a lot. I want to do for others what I'd like them to do for me. I know I can set a good example for other kids, but please help me to do that in a humble way, God. Amen.

. . . .

Can you think of specific times when you did not use good manners? What happened then compared to when you do choose to use good manners?

KINDNESS AT THE PARK

Be full of joy always because you belong to the Lord.
Again I say, be full of joy!
PHILIPPIANS 4:4

Dear God, thank You for cool parks where I get to run and be loud and climb and swing and play! It's fun to be a kid and use my imagination. I like to be with my friends at parks too so we can play together. Help me to see the opportunities for kindness when I'm playing at the park. I can pick up any litter I see and throw it away. I can take turns kindly on playground equipment. I can help younger kids if I see they need something. There are so many ways to show kindness and share Your love when I'm at the park. Please keep showing me the kind things You want me to do! Amen.

....

Where is your favorite park, and what is your
favorite thing to do there? Praise and
thank God for those blessings!

KINDNESS IN THE KITCHEN

So if you eat or drink or whatever you do,
do everything to honor God.

1 CORINTHIANS 10:31

Dear God, I always want to be looking for ways to share kindness at home, and one way is doing more in the kitchen. The older I get, the more I can do to cook and clean up, and I know that helps out Mom and Dad a lot! I already have some chores in the kitchen, but I could learn to do more with a good attitude. And then I could teach my younger siblings more too. We could even make a fun game out of it. I know You love cheerful givers, God, and I want to give and serve cheerfully (2 Corinthians 9:7). Amen.

What are your favorite foods you'd like to try to cook?

SAFE AND FREE

Teach your people to obey the leaders of their country.
They should be ready to do any good work. They must not
speak bad of anyone, and they must not argue.
They should be gentle and kind to all people.

TITUS 3:1–2

Dear God, I'm thankful for police and law enforcement officers who help keep our communities safe. Help me to show kindness to them by praying for their safety and protection and for their strength and encouragement. Help me to remember to thank them when I see them. I could also visit their workplaces and take cards or goodies to them. I'm blessed to live in a safe and free country. I want to show my gratitude and share Your kindness and love. Amen.

Would you ever want to be a police or law
enforcement officer? Why or why not?

KINDNESS TO CREATION

Christ made everything in the heavens and on the earth.
He made everything that is seen and things that are not seen.
He made all the powers of heaven. Everything was made
by Him and for Him. Christ was before all things.
All things are held together by Him.

COLOSSIANS 1:16–17

Dear God, I love Your beautiful creation! Help me to be wise about living in it without harming it. A lot of people in our world seem to worship our earth, and "being green" is almost like a religion to them. Help me to be kind to those people and point them to You and Your love more than love of the earth. I appreciate the earth that You, our Creator, have given us, but I want to worship You alone. Show me how to be kind to and respectful of this beautiful world You made for us. Amen.

....

What are your favorite animals and plants
in all of God's amazing creation?

WHEN SCHOOLWORK IS HARD

You should be happy when you have all kinds of tests. You know these prove your faith. It helps you not to give up. Learn well how to wait so you will be strong and complete and in need of nothing. If you do not have wisdom, ask God for it. He is always ready to give it to you and will never say you are wrong for asking. You must have faith as you ask Him. You must not doubt.

JAMES 1:2–6

Dear God, when I'm struggling with homework and just not understanding, please help me to be kind even in the midst of my frustration. Help me to have patience with myself, my teacher, my parents, my tutor, and anyone else who might be trying to help me. Help me to listen well to them and keep trying, even when I feel like giving up. Please give me wisdom and understanding as I try to learn new and hard things. Amen.

What are your hardest subjects in school?

WHEN SCHOOLWORK IS EASY

Do not let yourselves get tired of doing good. If we do not
give up, we will get what is coming to us at the right time.
Because of this, we should do good to everyone. For sure,
we should do good to those who belong to Christ.

GALATIANS 6:9–10

Dear God, when I know friends or younger siblings
are struggling with learning something for school, and
it's something I can do well, remind me to show kindness by being a good helper to them. I could sit down
and help tutor them or make up games for fun study
sessions. Thank You for the school subjects that come
easily for me! I want to help others understand them
well too.

....

What school subjects do you enjoy the
most or come the most easily to you?

KEEP COOL

He who is slow to anger is better than the powerful.
PROVERBS 16:32

Dear God, Your Word doesn't say I should never get angry. There are some things that *should* cause anger, like sin and things that hurt people and hurt You. If I see a bully hurting a classmate, that definitely should make me angry. Or if I hear someone telling lies about a friend, that should make me angry too! But Your Word does say I should be very careful with anger and the way I act when I'm angry. I need to keep cool, so I need lots of self-control when I feel angry. Controlling my anger well is a way to show kindness and respect to God, myself, and others. Please give me self-control when I'm feeling angry and wisdom for dealing with anger well. Thank You, God, for Your help! Amen.

What kinds of things make you feel especially angry?
What specific things can you do to stay
calm and deal with anger well?

LOOK FOR THE LONELY

Remember to do good and help each other.
Gifts like this please God.
HEBREWS 13:16

Dear God, help me to show kindness by looking around for the lonely. I want to notice others who seem like they could use a friend. Maybe during lunch or recess at school I see that a certain classmate is almost always alone. Give me courage to sit with her and invite her to talk and play with me. Or maybe I know an elderly person in my neighborhood who lives alone and needs company. Help me to start visiting with him, even if just on his front porch for a few minutes a week. Help me to see and love others as You do, God! Amen.

· ·

What do you appreciate when you feel lonely?
How can you share that kindness with others?

KINDNESS AT THE LIBRARY

A wise man will hear and grow in learning.
PROVERBS 1:5

Dear God, I am thankful for libraries! They are full of not just awesome books but many other resources and opportunities for fun activities for kids like me. Help me to show my appreciation well by being a good patron of libraries. Help me to treat the items I borrow kindly and of course to treat the employees of libraries kindly too! Help me to be kind to fellow patrons of the library by being respectful and quiet when I'm supposed to be. When I choose kindness and good behavior in simple things, I share Your love in little ways that make a big difference. Amen.

....

What are your favorite books
and activities at the library?

ORPHANS AND WIDOWS

Religion that is pure and good before God the Father is to help
children who have no parents and to care for women whose
husbands have died who have troubles. Pure religion is also
to keep yourself clean from the sinful things of the world.

JAMES 1:27

Dear God, I think it's awesome when people adopt or foster kids who need homes and families! Please help me be extra kind and helpful to families who have adopted or who take care of foster children. Give me ideas for things I can do for them and ways I can encourage them. Please help me do the same for moms who are raising their kids alone. Help me to be kind and a good friend to kids I know who are adopted or in foster care or who have only one parent at home. Especially help me to share with them how much You love and care for them. Amen.

• •

What adoption stories do you know?
What inspires you about them?

SHARING GOD'S WORD

All the Holy Writings are God-given and are made alive by Him. Man is helped when he is taught God's Word. It shows what is wrong. It changes the way of a man's life. It shows him how to be right with God. It gives the man who belongs to God everything he needs to work well for Him.

2 TIMOTHY 3:16–17

Dear God, please help me to spend time reading the Bible and memorizing scripture. I can share great kindness with others when I'm full of scriptures to share with them and point them to. Your Word is our guide for life! It's so great to have to help us in everything. It's how You speak to us. Help me to have a huge love for Your Word, God, and to share that love with others. Amen.

What are your favorite scripture verses?

KINDNESS = HAPPINESS!

Happy is the man who cares for the poor. The Lord will save him in times of trouble. The Lord will keep him alive and safe. And he will be happy upon the earth. You will not give him over to the desire of those who hate him. The Lord will give him strength on his bed of sickness. When he is sick, You will make him well again.

PSALM 41:1–3

Dear God, I want to remember all the time how much You appreciate and reward kindness. You love when Your people take care of the poor and the sick and the needy. You bless us when we do. You fill us with joy and happiness for doing what You've called us to do. Nothing tops that! I thank You and praise You for these good opportunities to share kindness. Amen.

....

How do you feel inside when you
show kindness and help others?

LONG-TERM MISSIONARY

*"Go and make followers of all the nations. Baptize them in
the name of the Father and of the Son and of the Holy
Spirit. Teach them to do all the things I have told you.
And I am with you always, even to the end of the world."*

MATTHEW 28:19–20

Dear God, Your Son, Jesus, commanded us to go and
make followers of Him all over the world. I want to
be a good follower of You wherever I am, and I want
to be an example showing others how to do that too.
I can spread Your kindness by being a missionary everywhere I go. God, I know some people go and live
as missionaries in foreign countries to help make more
followers of You. Please give them extra kindness, protection, and blessings! Living and serving in a foreign
land can't be easy. Help me to remember to think of
them and pray for them. Amen.

Have you ever met any missionaries to foreign countries
and heard their stories? What inspired you about them?

SHORT-TERM MISSIONARY

*"But you will receive power when the Holy Spirit comes into
your life. You will tell about Me in the city of Jerusalem and
over all the countries of Judea and Samaria
and to the ends of the earth."*

ACTS 1:8

Dear God, please help me to know if You would want
me to go on a mission trip soon or maybe someday in
the future. I know churches organize special trips that
even kids like me can participate in. The service that
people do on those trips shares great kindness with
the people they visit and care for. If You are asking me
to do this, please give me guidance and support and
wisdom. Thank You, God! Amen.

Have you ever gone on a mission trip?
Where did you go, and what did you do?

KINDNESS TO MOMS AND BABIES

You put me together inside my mother. I will give thanks to You, for the greatness of the way I was made brings fear. Your works are great and my soul knows it very well.

PSALM 139:13–14

Dear God, it's amazing how You created babies to grow and be cared for first in their moms' tummies. Help me to show kindness and love to women who are expecting babies. I can do simple things like holding doors for them at stores or offering to carry bags for them. If a grown-up friend or family member is pregnant, I can ask if I can do anything to help her. And I can see if there are ways I can help at local pregnancy centers. You love babies and children and their mothers so much, God, and I want to love them like You do too! Amen.

How was your mom shown kindness and help when she carried you in her tummy? What is the story of the day you were born?

IN EVERY SEASON

"While the earth lasts, planting time and gathering time, cold and heat, summer and winter, and day and night will not end."
GENESIS 8:22

Dear God, I love how You created our world with different seasons. Winter is so fun for playing in the snow. Spring brings such pretty flowers and warmth again. Summertime is just the best for swimming and playing outside until late at night. And fall is amazing with the trees turning beautiful colors plus all the fun and yumminess of pumpkin patches, corn mazes, apple cider, and donuts. Please help me to show kindness to my family and friends and neighbors by helping out in every season. There are driveways to shovel in winter, yards to prepare in spring, lawns to mow in summer, and leaves to rake in the fall. There are all kinds of ways I can help out and share kindness in every beautiful season. Thank You, God, for all of them! Amen.

Which season is your favorite and why?

LISTEN A LOT

Everyone should listen much and speak little.
He should be slow to become angry.

JAMES 1:19

Dear God, sometimes I get into big arguments with siblings or friends or even my parents. I say mean things that I shouldn't. Sometimes the words just pop out of my mouth when I'm feeling angry or upset. I wish I could take them back, but I can't. No wonder Your Word says everyone should listen a lot and speak only a little. Please help me to show kindness by thinking before I speak and watching what I say when I'm angry or upset. If I do mess up and say ugly things, please help me to say I'm sorry quickly and work to make things right. I need a lot of help with this, God, but I know You are working powerfully in me. Thank You! Amen.

....

When do you find it hardest to control your words?
How can you ask God to help you with that more?

A MIND FULL OF KINDNESS

Keep your minds thinking about whatever is true, whatever is respected, whatever is right, whatever is pure, whatever can be loved, and whatever is well thought of.

PHILIPPIANS 4:8

Dear God, Philippians 4:8 is such a great scripture to memorize and put on repeat in my brain. So many awful things in this world can steal my attention and put bad thoughts in my mind. Help me to keep them all out! If I want to share kindness, I need a mind filled with exactly what's listed here in this scripture—what is true, respected, right, pure, lovable, and well thought of. If my mind is full of those things, then how could kindness not overflow from me in my attitude and actions? Thank You that if we do what Your Word says, we are wise, because You help us live the best, most rewarding life possible! Amen.

· ·

What kinds of things do you need to avoid to keep bad thoughts from entering your mind?

REAL LOVE

Love does not give up. Love is kind. Love is not jealous.
Love does not put itself up as being important. Love has no
pride. Love does not do the wrong thing. Love never thinks
of itself. Love does not get angry. Love does not remember
the suffering that comes from being hurt by someone.
Love is not happy with sin. Love is happy with the
truth. Love takes everything that comes without giving
up. Love believes all things. Love hopes for all things.
Love keeps on in all things. Love never comes to an end.

1 Corinthians 13:4–8

Dear God, the world spreads a lot of ideas of what love is that sure don't seem to match up with what You say love is and what You have shown love is. I want to learn it from You, not the world. Please help me, and then please help me to spread kindness by demonstrating Your love and helping teach others what it is. Amen.

What differences have you seen in what the world says love is and what God says love is?

ASK THE ANIMALS

"But ask the wild animals, and they will teach you. Ask the birds of the heavens, and let them tell you. Or speak to the earth, and let it teach you. Let the fish of the sea make it known to you. Who among all these does not know that the hand of the Lord has done this? In His hand is the life of every living thing and the breath of all men."

JOB 12:7–10

Dear God, when I see someone discouraged, wondering if they should believe in You or not, help me to kindly share with them the truth that is found in this scripture. You remind us so well in all of Your creation how real and awesome You are! You are our loving Creator, and I praise You and want everyone to know and love You! Amen.

What is most amazing to you about God's creation?

KINDNESS TO GOVERNMENT LEADERS

*First of all, I ask you to pray much for all men and to give thanks
for them. Pray for kings and all others who are in power over us
so we might live quiet God-like lives in peace. It is good when
you pray like this. It pleases God Who is the One Who saves.
He wants all people to be saved from the punishment of
sin. He wants them to come to know the truth.*

1 TIMOTHY 2:1–4

Dear God, I don't always understand when I hear
grown-ups talking about politics. I do know it can
sure make people upset! Help me to share kindness by
gently reminding people that no matter what we feel
about politics, Your Word tells us to pray for people
in power. We make You happy when we do. Mostly
we need to pray for all people to be saved from sin
like You want. Thank You for sending our Savior, Jesus
Christ! Amen.

What interests or confuses you about
government and politics?

BIRTHDAY FUN

*Your eyes saw me before I was put together. And all the days of
my life were written in Your book before any of them came to be.*
PSALM 139:16

Dear God, thank You for birthdays! Help me to show
kindness to others on their birthdays by simply telling them happy birthday and that I'm glad You created them. Help me to remember to make a card for
friends, classmates, family members, and other loved
ones on their birthdays. It's such a simple and fun way
to be kind. On my own birthday, help me to be full of
grace and gratitude and not greediness. I love parties
and celebrations for birthdays, God! Help me to use
birthdays as a way to spread Your kindness and love!
Amen.

What is your favorite thing about your birthday?
What do you love about others' birthdays?

ALL FEARS AWAY

Give great honor to the Lord with me. Let us praise His name together. I looked for the Lord, and He answered me. And He took away all my fears.

Psalm 34:3–4

Dear God, please help me with my fears. Please take them away from me. Some seem silly, and others are pretty big and awful. But if I focus on how great You are, how much You love me and provide for me, and how much I can praise You, I won't have time to think about fear and You will take it all away from me. God, when my fears are gone, I have more time and energy to spread kindness to others. Help me to share with everyone around me about how You can take all fears away! Thank You! Amen.

What are some specific fears you
need to let God take away?

STOP THE GOSSIP

*He who watches over his mouth and his
tongue keeps his soul from troubles.*

PROVERBS 21:23

Dear God, please help me never to join in with gossip. If I hear it, help me to shut it down or walk away from the conversation. You want people to encourage each other and build each other up, not tear each other down. I never want to be the subject of gossip, and I never want to participate in it about others either. Help me to show kindness by being the one who stops the spread of gossip any chance I get. This task isn't easy, God! Please help me to be brave and strong. Amen.

Have you ever joined in with gossip? How did you feel compared to how you feel when you encourage someone in a good and kind way?

BE KIND ANYWAY

*"You are happy when people act and talk in a bad way to you
and make it very hard for you and tell bad things and lies about
you because you trust in Me. Be glad and full of joy
because your reward will be much in heaven."*

MATTHEW 5:11–12

Dear God, my Christian friends and I sometimes get made fun of for believing in You and loving You. Help us to be kind anyway. Your Word says we should be glad and full of joy because we'll be rewarded in heaven for this kind of thing. It doesn't feel like a happy thing right in the moment to be mistreated because of living for You, but I never want to reject You! If we focus on the blessings You give for going through it, then we can be happy. You are always good and kind, God, no matter how You are being treated! Help me to be too! Amen.

Have you ever been made fun of by other kids?
Describe how you felt.

WHEN KINDNESS DOESN'T FEEL NICE

There is no joy while we are being punished. It is hard to take,
but later we can see that good came from it. And it
gives us the peace of being right with God.

HEBREWS 12:11

Dear God, help me to remember that kindness doesn't always feel nice and warm and cozy. For example, I might not always agree in the moment, but when I really think about it, my parents are always being kind when they discipline me. Obviously, consequences and punishment for bad behavior are not fun. They might even feel totally awful at first, but actually my parents are kind to teach me respect and responsibility. Help me to accept the kindness of discipline with a good attitude. Also, God, I need guidance from You to know when to share kindness with others by telling them things that might be hard to hear but really are for their good in the long run. Please help me to have wisdom in this area all of my life. Amen.

....

What have you learned from good
discipline so far in your life?

HONESTLY KIND

We want to do the right thing.
We want God and men to know we are honest.

2 CORINTHIANS 8:21

Dear God, help me to remember that being honest is always a way to show kindness. In big things and in little things, the truth matters. Lies are never good for anyone and only bring trouble. I want to be a trustworthy kid who becomes a trustworthy adult. I sure appreciate grown-ups I can trust and depend on, and the way to become one is to start now. I want to love the truth and have integrity in everything I do. Please help me to be honest constantly, God! Amen.

Have you ever lied and then the lie was discovered?
How did you feel? Or have you ever been tempted
to lie but decided not to? What happened?

SHINING LIGHT

If you give what you have to the hungry, and fill the needs of
those who suffer, then your light will rise in the darkness, and
your darkness will be like the brightest time of day. The Lord will
always lead you. He will meet the needs of your soul in the dry
times and give strength to your body. You will be like a garden
that has enough water, like a well of water that never dries up.

ISAIAH 58:10–11

Dear God, this scripture reminds me that giving to
the needy and providing for those who are suffering
are the things that make my light shine. You promise
You will always meet my needs as I help to meet the
needs of others. You give me a constant filling up with
kindness and love so I can constantly pour out kindness and love to others. You're amazing, God! Keep on
leading me and filling me, please. Amen.

....

What are specific ways God fills you up with
love so you can share love with others?

SERVICE DOGS

*God will give you everything you need because
of His great riches in Christ Jesus.*

PHILIPPIANS 4:19

Dear God, I love to see service dogs helping their owners. You are so awesome to have created animals that can help people with special needs! Help me to be respectful of these dogs and their owners. I would love to pet and play with these dogs, but I know I need to be respectful of the job they do and realize that I might be too much of a distraction to them. Please help me only to touch a service dog if I have been given permission. Otherwise I just need to watch and appreciate them! Dogs are amazing, God! Thank You for them! Amen.

· ·

Do you know any people who have a service dog?
How do they inspire you?

ALWAYS READY

But even if you suffer for doing what is right, you will be happy.
Do not be afraid or troubled by what they may do to make it
hard for you. Your heart should be holy and set apart for the Lord
God. Always be ready to tell everyone who asks you why you
believe as you do. Be gentle as you speak and show respect.

1 Peter 3:14–15

Dear God, please help me to be someone who always wants to do what is right, even if I know it will be hard or embarrassing. I want to live the way You want me to, God, not to make others happy—just You! Help me always to be ready to tell others why I love You and want to live for You. And help me to do it in kind ways that make people want to know more and more about You. Amen.

Are you always ready to share your faith in Jesus?
How do you prepare?

NEVER TOO YOUNG

Let no one show little respect for you because you are young.
Show other Christians how to live by your life. They should be
able to follow you in the way you talk and in what you do.
Show them how to live in faith and in love and in holy living.

1 TIMOTHY 4:12

Dear God, sometimes because I'm young—and can't drive to go places or get a regular job to have much money—I start to think there aren't a lot of things I can do to share with others. But remind me it's silly to think that way. I can show kindness every day, wherever I am, no matter my age. I just want to serve You and share Your kindness and love wherever You put me and with whatever good things You give me, God. Please constantly show me what You want me to do! Amen.

Do you ever feel unimportant or like you can't do
much because you are young? Will you fight
that lie with the truth from 1 Timothy 4:12?

LOADS OF LOVE

Most of all, have a true love for each other.
Love covers many sins.

1 PETER 4:8

Dear God, I know some kids who, while they aren't mean bullies, are still really hard to be around because they're just obnoxious and annoying. I don't want to say that about them to other kids because I don't want to gossip or be mean. But I need to vent it to You, God! Please help me to know how to be kind to them even when it's hard! I'm not perfect and I can act obnoxious and annoying sometimes too, so I need to give them patience and grace like I need others to give me sometimes. You, God, are the very best at giving patience and grace. You love every person unconditionally, no matter how obnoxiously we might be acting. Please give me wisdom for dealing with difficult people. I need loads of Your kind of love to give to others. Help me to be like You. Amen.

. . . .

How has God helped you deal with difficult people?

TAKING AWAY TEARS

"God will take away all their tears. There will be no more death or sorrow or crying or pain. All the old things have passed away." Then the One sitting on the throne said, "See! I am making all things new."

REVELATION 21:4–5

Dear God, I love this scripture reminding me that one day there will be no more death or sadness or pain. You are making all things new, and everyone who trusts in Your Son, Jesus Christ, as their Savior will live forever in perfect paradise with You someday. Help me to share kindness with others by reminding them of this truth again and again, especially when someone is sad or in pain. Thank You for caring about our tears, God. Thank You that You are working to get rid of them forever. Amen.

In addition to sharing scripture, what are other specific ways you can show kindness when someone is crying or sad?

BE QUIET

Be quiet and know that I am God. I will be honored among the nations. I will be honored in the earth. The Lord of All is with us. The God of Jacob is our strong place.

PSALM 46:10–11

Dear God, I could spend oodles of time asking You for help with choosing kindness, but I also need to make sure I'm taking time to stop and be quiet and listen after I ask for Your help. I listen by being quiet before You and trusting You as God Almighty who has power over everything and everyone. I listen by reading Your Word and learning from it and from people I know and trust who love You and live for You. I listen by letting praise songs speak to me. I listen by quietly serving You. Help me to be still before You, God. I can only grow in kindness and love by being ready and willing to hear from You. Amen.

What are the specific ways you
quiet yourself before God?

THE GREATEST LAWS

"Teacher, which one is the greatest of the Laws?" Jesus said to him, " 'You must love the Lord your God with all your heart and with all your soul and with all your mind.' This is the first and greatest of the Laws. The second is like it, 'You must love your neighbor as you love yourself.' All the Laws and the writings of the early preachers depend on these two most important Laws."

MATTHEW 22:36–40

Dear God, this scripture in Matthew 22 is exactly what I need to focus on for choosing kindness. If I am loving You with all my heart, soul, and mind, and loving others as I love myself, I can't help but be kind to others. Help me to memorize this scripture and live it out all of my days. Amen.

What does it mean to love God with all your heart, soul, and mind?

UNCHANGING COMFORT

Lord, You have been the place of comfort for all people of all time.
Before the mountains were born, before You gave birth to
the earth and the world, forever and ever, You are God.

PSALM 90:1–2

Dear God, I like to take a deep, relaxing breath as I read this scripture. You are my place of comfort, just as You have been for all people through all the ages. You are everlasting, and You don't change (Malachi 3:6). In a world where things are changing every day (and that can feel scary sometimes!), I love that You stay the same. You are always here for me and offer me a constant place of peace and strength and comfort. And never just for me alone, but for everyone. Thank You for this kindness. Help me to tell others how You offer it to them too! Amen.

What do you picture as you think
of God as your place of comfort?

KINDNESS AND GENEROSITY

Remember, the man who plants only a few seeds will not have much grain to gather. The man who plants many seeds will have much grain to gather. Each man should give as he has decided in his heart. He should not give, wishing he could keep it. Or he should not give if he feels he has to give. God loves a man who gives because he wants to give. God can give you all you need. He will give you more than enough. You will have everything you need for yourselves. And you will have enough left over to give when there is a need.

2 CORINTHIANS 9:6–8

God, help me always to be kind and generous with everything I have, starting now when I'm a kid and continuing when I'm a grown-up. Your Word promises that the more I give to others, the more You give to me. Please give me a heart like Yours, God! Amen.

In what areas do you struggle to be generous? How can you ask God to help you?

HEAVENLY BODIES

Our body is like a house we live in here on earth. When it is destroyed, we know that God has another body for us in heaven. The new one will not be made by human hands as a house is made. This body will last forever. Right now we cry inside ourselves because we wish we could have our new body which we will have in heaven. We will not be without a body. We will live in a new body.

2 Corinthians 5:1–3

Dear God, I think this is one of the most comforting scriptures You have given for anyone who is sad about the death of a loved one. You promise that if anyone trusts in Jesus as Savior, then You have a new home and body and eternal life waiting for them in heaven when they leave this earth. Help me to share this truth and hope with anyone I know who is grieving because someone they loved has died. Amen.

How do you picture our new heavenly bodies?

FAITHFUL

"Know then that the Lord your God is God, the faithful God.
He keeps His promise and shows His loving-kindness to
those who love Him and keep His Laws, even to
a thousand family groups in the future."

DEUTERONOMY 7:9

Dear God, thank You for being faithful to people, even when we are not always faithful to You. We hurt ourselves and each other by not being faithful. Help us to be more like You! Help me to share the truth of Your faithfulness with family and friends who feel betrayed by people who were not faithful to them. We all need to look to You as our one and only source of absolute faithfulness, because no person is perfect and You are the only One who never lets us down. You are so kind in Your faithfulness to us, God! Thank You! Amen.

What are specific ways you have seen God show
His faithfulness to you and your family?

MAKE WEAK FAITH STRONGER

"If You can do anything to help us, take pity on us!" Jesus said to him, "Why do you ask Me that? The one who has faith can do all things." At once the father cried out. He said with tears in his eyes, "Lord, I have faith. Help my weak faith to be stronger!"

MARK 9:22–24

Dear God, like the father in this scripture, I believe in You but sometimes I need You to make my faith stronger. Help me to remember that I can always ask You for stronger faith. Help me to remind others that they can too. You are so kind to answer us and strengthen us.

....

Have you had times when your faith felt weak?
How did God make it stronger?

GOD'S WORK AND OUR WORK

We are His work. He has made us to belong to Christ Jesus so we can work for Him. He planned that we should do this.

EPHESIANS 2:10

Dear God, please help me just to do what You want me to do every day. You have specific plans and purposes for me. When I do the things You've created for me, I'm totally sharing Your love and kindness with others because You've designed each person uniquely with different gifts to serve and help each other (1 Peter 4:10–11). I want to wake up each day asking You, "How do You want me to work for You today, God? Help me to do it well to praise You." Amen.

What do you think are the specific gifts God gave you to use to serve Him? Ask Him to keep showing You and teaching You.

GOOD AND KIND AND NEAR

*The Lord is right and good in all His ways, and kind in all
His works. The Lord is near to all who call on
Him, to all who call on Him in truth.*

PSALM 145:17–18

Dear God, I'm grateful for this scripture that reminds
me how good You are in all Your ways, in everything
You do! Thank You for always being near to those who
call on You in truth. It's amazing that You are the one
true sovereign Creator God of the entire universe, and
yet You are near to each one of us individually! Remind me of this truth daily, and help me to remind
others of it too! You are so good and kind, God! Amen.

....

What does it mean to call on God in truth?

NEVER GIVE UP!

Do not let yourselves get tired of doing good. If we do not give up, we will get what is coming to us at the right time. Because of this, we should do good to everyone. For sure, we should do good to those who belong to Christ.

GALATIANS 6:9–10

Dear God, sometimes I feel totally overwhelmed by all the kindness needed by so many people in the world. There is so much sadness and pain everywhere. I feel like there is so much to do that my efforts will never be enough. Sometimes I wonder if I should even try! Remind me that a defeated feeling is a lie that comes from my enemy, Satan, and he wants me to quit trying to show Your kindness and love. He would love for me to be selfish and mean and never think about others. I want to win over his lies and cruelty, God! Help me to defeat him by never giving up in sharing kindness and love. Amen.

....

What are the things that make you feel defeated sometimes? Keep asking God to help you win over them!

A LOT FROM A LITTLE

"There is a boy here who has five loaves of barley bread and two small fish. What is that for so many people?" Jesus said, "Have the people sit down." There was much grass in that place. About five thousand men sat down. . . . The people had as much as they wanted. When they were filled, Jesus said to His followers, "Gather up the pieces that are left. None will be wasted." The followers gathered the pieces together. Twelve baskets were filled with pieces of barley bread.

JOHN 6:9–13

Dear God, I love the story of the miracle of the boy with the five loaves and two fish—how You turned his small offering into *so much more!* Amazing! I pray you do that with what I have to give, God! I'm just a kid and don't always have a lot I can do, but please take the love and kindness I do have to offer and multiply them big time! Amen.

How have you seen God take something small and turn it into something more?

SHOW PEOPLE WHEN THEY ARE WRONG

Preach the Word of God. Preach it when it is easy and people want to listen and when it is hard and people do not want to listen. Preach it all the time. Use the Word of God to show people they are wrong. Use the Word of God to help them do right. You must be willing to wait for people to understand what you teach as you teach them.

2 TIMOTHY 4:2

Dear God, this scripture reminds us it's kind to keep sharing Your Word all the time, even when it's hard, even when people don't want to listen. It's kind to show people when they are doing wrong, not just go along with anything to keep them happy. Please give me courage and wisdom to help others do what is right, God. And help me to be teachable too when others need to show me what I'm doing wrong. Amen.

Has there been a time when you needed to show someone what they were doing wrong, according to God's Word? How did it go?

NO FEAR

For God did not give us a spirit of fear. He gave us a spirit of power and of love and of a good mind. Do not be ashamed to tell others about what our Lord said, or of me here in prison. I am here because of Jesus Christ. Be ready to suffer for preaching the Good News and God will give you the strength you need.

2 Timothy 1:7–8

Dear God, I can't show kindness if I'm too afraid to reach out to others or too afraid to share the Good News about Your Son, Jesus. Help me to remember You have not given us a spirit of fear. You have given us power and love and good minds, and we have no reason to be ashamed of You! We might suffer like Paul did in the Bible, but You will help us through any kind of struggle and pain, and You will reward us greatly for sharing Your love and kindness no matter what. Amen.

What are your fears about reaching
out to others with God's love?

PEACEMAKERS

"Watch yourselves! If your brother sins, speak sharp words to him. If he is sorry and turns from his sin, forgive him."

LUKE 17:3

Dear God, Your Word says peacemakers are blessed, and sometimes it seems like we mess up what that means. It doesn't mean there should never be any conflict and everyone has to be sugary sweet all the time. Sometimes some conflict is necessary before peace can happen. Take standing up to a bully, for instance. There can be a kind of peace if everyone always gives in to a bully, but that's not a good peace. Real peace comes only when the bully stops bullying! Help me not to be afraid of good conflict. Help me to confront others bravely when it's for their good and the good of others. I need Your wisdom for this, God. Thank You for giving it! Amen.

Have you ever confronted someone in order to bring peace to a situation? If so, how did it go?

SAFE PLACE

*God is our safe place and our strength. He is always our help
when we are in trouble. So we will not be afraid, even if the
earth is shaken and the mountains fall into the center of the
sea, and even if its waters go wild with storm
and the mountains shake with its action.*

PSALM 46:1–3

Dear God, no matter what is going on anytime, anywhere, You are our safe place and strength. You are our
help in any kind of trouble. We don't have to be afraid
of anything, even crazy-sounding things like mountains
falling into the center of the sea! Help me to remember this reassuring scripture and to kindly share it with
others I know who are struggling with fear. Amen.

....

What causes fear in you or in some of your friends?

KEEP GOING THE RIGHT WAY

My Christian brothers, if any of you should be led away from the truth, let someone turn him back again. That person should know that if he turns a sinner from the wrong way, he will save the sinner's soul from death and many sins will be forgiven.

JAMES 5:19–20

Dear God, help me to show kindness by being someone who pulls people away from living a sinful life and toward following You! We all need other people to help us keep going the right way—the way You guide us in Your Word, God. Help me never to reject You. Instead, help me to follow You closely and to help others find their way back to You! Amen.

Have you ever pulled someone away
from sin and toward Jesus?

KIND WARNINGS

Keep awake! Watch at all times. The devil is working against
you. He is walking around like a hungry lion with
his mouth open. He is looking for someone to eat.
Stand against him and be strong in your faith.

1 PETER 5:8–9

Dear God, some people seem to want to think of You and the Bible as only happy, warm, fuzzy, loving feelings. But sometimes love and kindness mean listening to hard things and warnings—like how we have an unseen enemy called the devil or Satan who constantly works against us. He's like a hungry wild animal ready to destroy us. That thought is scary, but I want to remember it and warn people about him. We need to stay strong in our faith in You, God, so we can be strong against our enemy. Please help us and protect us! Amen.

What are specific ways you are working to stay strong
in your faith so you can stand against the devil?

ANOTHER WARNING

*He will punish those who do not know God and those who do
not obey the Good News of our Lord Jesus Christ. They will be
punished forever and taken away from the Lord and
from the shining-greatness of His power.*

2 THESSALONIANS 1:8–9

Dear God, another kind warning of Yours is about hell. It's a real and awful place, and it's punishment for anyone who does not believe in You as the one and only Savior from sin. You love us so deeply and want so much for no one to go to hell that You sent Your only Son to take on our sin and shame and die in our place to make a way for us to live with You in perfect heaven instead of hell. Help me to be kind and warn others about hell. Help me to tell them about Your great love offered through Your Son, Jesus, to save them and give them eternal life! Amen.

Who in your life needs a loving
and kind warning about hell?

LOOKING UP TO OTHERS

*I will praise You, my God and King. I will honor Your name
forever and ever. I will honor You every day, and praise Your
name forever and ever. The Lord is great and our praise to
Him should be great. He is too great for anyone to understand.
Families of this time will praise Your works to the families-
to-come. They will tell about Your powerful acts.*

PSALM 145:1–4

Dear God, I am so grateful for Christian role models
and mentors in my life. They show their kindness by
striving to help me grow into a good and responsible adult who loves and lives for You. As I'm growing,
please help me to watch for those younger than me
who might be looking up to me as a mentor in their
lives. I want to return the kindness that good mentors
have shown me. Amen.

Who are your mentors and role models, and why?

GOD'S GREAT POWER

The voice of the Lord is upon the waters. The God of shining-greatness thunders. The Lord is over many waters. The voice of the Lord is powerful. The voice of the Lord is great. The voice of the Lord breaks the cedars.

PSALM 29:3–5

Dear God, I love to read scriptures about Your power. They remind me that no problem of mine is too big for You to help with. Thank You that You are almighty over every person and all of creation, and You also care about me and everything I care about. Wow! Help me to share about Your power and might with others. I can spread kindness by reminding people that You are greater and stronger than any hard thing we are going through! You love to help us, and we thank and praise You! Amen.

....

What hard things do You need God's power and help for right now? Who in your life needs to be reminded of God's great power?

LOOK TO JESUS

Do not love the world or anything in the world. If anyone loves the world, the Father's love is not in him. For everything that is in the world does not come from the Father. The desires of our flesh and the things our eyes see and want and the pride of this life come from the world. The world and all its desires will pass away. But the man who obeys God and does what He wants done will live forever.

1 JOHN 2:15–17

Dear God, if I try to be like the world, I will never have the kindness and love that You do. I don't want to follow what the world says I should do. I want to constantly look to You (Hebrews 12:2). I love that old song that says, "Turn your eyes upon Jesus. Look full in His wonderful face. And the things of earth will grow strangely dim, in the light of your glory and grace." I want to constantly watch for and see You, Jesus! Amen.

Do you feel like your eyes are focused on Jesus? What steps can you take to improve your focus on Him?

LIVE IN THE LIGHT AND
SHARE WITH EACH OTHER

If we live in the light as He is in the light,
we share what we have in God with each other.

1 JOHN 1:7

Dear God, as I form friendships with others, please help me to be a friend who includes others. I don't want to be part of cliquey groups that exclude others or won't get to know others. Your kindness draws people in rather than shuts them out. I want to draw others in too. I want to live in the light as You are in the light. Please help me and my friends to share what we have in You with each other, like Your Word says. Amen.

Have you ever been excluded? How did that make you feel? How can you work to include others who need kindness and love?

NO WORRIES

"I tell you this: Do not worry about your life. Do not worry about what you are going to eat and drink. Do not worry about what you are going to wear. Is not life more important than food? Is not the body more important than clothes? Look at the birds in the sky. They do not plant seeds. They do not gather grain. They do not put grain into a building to keep. Yet your Father in heaven feeds them! Are you not more important than the birds?"

MATTHEW 6:25–26

Dear God, even as a kid I sometimes worry about the future because I hear grown-ups worrying about it so much. Please give me wisdom for knowing how to prepare for the future, using the gifts You have given me, while at the same time not worrying about it at all. Help me to live well day by day, serving You and trusting that You will take care of all my needs when I'm following closely after You. Help me to share this truth and peace with others too. Amen.

....

What are the most common worries you hear of?

CHILD OF GOD

The person who believes that Jesus is the Christ is a child of God.
The person who loves the Father loves His children also. This is
the way we know we love God's children. It is when we love
God and obey His Word. Loving God means to obey
His Word, and His Word is not hard to obey.

1 JOHN 5:1–3

Dear God, You are so kind to allow me to be Your child! You make me royalty because You are the King of all kings (Revelation 19:16). Amazing! I never want to forget the incredible kindness You have shown me. Constantly remembering that You are my heavenly Father and I am Yours because You love me is what motivates me to show kindness and love to others. You are so good to me, God. Thank You! Amen.

How do you regularly remind yourself that
you are a much-loved child of God?

GOOD GROUP WORK

Be happy in your hope. Do not give up when trouble comes.
Do not let anything stop you from praying. Share what you have
with Christian brothers who are in need. Give meals and a
place to stay to those who need it. Pray and give thanks for those
who make trouble for you. Yes, pray for them instead of talking
against them. Be happy with those who are happy.
Be sad with those who are sad. Live in peace with
each other. Do not act or think with pride.

ROMANS 12:12–16

Dear God, when my friends or my siblings and I are trying to figure out what to do together or how to share something, I sometimes act so selfishly. It has happened during a group project at school too. I want others to do exactly what I say we should do, or I want all the best things for myself. Please help me to work on my attitude. I want to be fair and show kindness as we compromise and work things out well together. Amen.

When do you feel like you act most selfishly?
How can you choose to improve?

GRATEFUL PRAISE

Call out with joy to the Lord, all the earth. Be glad as you serve the Lord. Come before Him with songs of joy. Know that the Lord is God. It is He Who made us, and not we ourselves. We are His people and the sheep of His field. Go into His gates giving thanks and into His holy place with praise. Give thanks to Him. Honor His name. For the Lord is good. His loving-kindness lasts forever. And He is faithful to all people and to all their children-to-come.

PSALM 100

Dear God, I have so many reasons to praise You and be grateful! Help me to focus all the time on who You are and all that I have because of You! I want to constantly say thank You! Your loving-kindness is without end, and I want to become more and more like You each day. Amen.

· ·

What does it mean for all the earth
to call out with joy to the Lord?

NOT FAR FROM EACH ONE OF US

"The God Who made the world and everything in it is the Lord of heaven and earth. . . . He set the times and places where they should live. They were to look for God. Then they might feel after Him and find Him because He is not far from each one of us. It is in Him that we live and move and keep on living."

ACTS 17:24, 26–28

Dear God, I have a friend who is missing her family member who is far away. I can't replace that person in her life, but I want to help her through her sadness. Please help me to encourage her and figure out things we can do together that will comfort her. Thank You that You are never far from each one of us. You are with me, You are with my friend, and You are with the loved one my friend is missing so much. In that way, we are all close together because of You! Thank You, God, for loving each one of us and being near to us. Amen.

....

What helps comfort you when you're missing someone?

REALLY LOOKING GOOD

But the Lord said. . . , "Do not look at the way he looks on the outside or how tall he is, because I have not chosen him. For the Lord does not look at the things man looks at. A man looks at the outside of a person, but the Lord looks at the heart."

1 SAMUEL 16:7

Dear God, if I live my life with this scripture passage in mind, I can't help but share kindness. I should never focus most of my attention on how people look on the outside. I should focus on what their heart and spirit look like in Your eyes. Those are really the things that matter most—and they will lead me to treat others with the kind of love and respect they deserve. Amen.

What things of this world make us get too caught up in outward appearance?

SEE LIKE JESUS

Jesus saw her crying. The Jews who came with her were crying also. His heart was very sad and He was troubled.

JOHN 11:33

Dear Jesus, help me to see people like You see them. You see and love each and every one of us, and You know all the unique things that make us different. You also know all the hard stuff going on inside a person's heart and mind. Help me especially to see the good in others who seem sad or discouraged or anxious or left out. Give me courage to reach out to them. Help me to know the right things to say and do to show them kindness and encourage them.

....

Have you ever reached out to a discouraged friend when you didn't know what was wrong? How did God help?

READY TO SHARE

Tell them to do good and be rich in good works. They should give much to those in need and be ready to share. Then they will be gathering together riches for themselves.

1 TIMOTHY 6:18–19

Dear God, I like my stuff—toys, clothes, games, collections. Can You help me not to be greedy about stuff, though? I know I shouldn't want more, more, more and all the newest cool stuff that my friends have, but I admit I struggle with this. Help me to hold on to gifts loosely. Make me willing to share my stuff with others and to donate things when I have more than enough. Help me to be content with having just what I need. When I'm blessed with even more than I need, help me to really appreciate that and then ask what You want me to do with the extras. I realize that being willing to let go of things if You ask me to is the way I make room for You to give me the new blessings You want to give. Amen.

....

Have you ever shared something even though sharing felt hard, but then God blessed you even more because of it?

HEALER AND SAVIOR

*Praise the Lord, O my soul. And all that is within me, praise His
holy name. Praise the Lord, O my soul. And forget none of His
acts of kindness. He forgives all my sins. He heals all my diseases.
He saves my life from the grave. He crowns me with loving-
kindness and pity. He fills my years with good things
and I am made young again like the eagle.*

PSALM 103:1–5

Dear God, You give me so much kindness! Thank You!
When I know of a friend or family member who is
sick and needs healing, help me remember to share
this scripture with them. You heal and You save, and
You alone can do that. Whether here on earth or one
day in heaven, You will heal everyone from every kind
of disease and death. I have so much hope in You, and
I want to share it with everyone. I praise You! Amen.

....

What does it mean to be made
young again like the eagle?

WHY SO BLUE?

*Why are you sad, O my soul? Why have you become troubled
within me? Hope in God, for I will praise Him
again, my help and my God.*

PSALM 43:5

Dear God, sometimes I get in a terrible mood for no reason at all. It's like I can't pull myself out of a funk, and I feel mad and sad all at once. Please help me figure out where those feelings are coming from. Help me to be willing to talk out those feelings with a grown-up I love and trust. I want to be wise and kind to myself in those times, and then I want to help others who might be feeling blue too. I sure need Your help, though, God. Thank You for giving it! Amen.

....

Who are the grown-ups in your life whom you
and your siblings and friends can always trust
for good advice and conversation?

CHANGE YOUR LIFE

Do not act like the sinful people of the world. Let God change your life. First of all, let Him give you a new mind. Then you will know what God wants you to do. And the things you do will be good and pleasing and perfect.

ROMANS 12:2

Dear God, please help me to live differently in this world. So many kids my age are just trying to fit in. Yes, I want to form good friendships, but not by being exactly like everyone else. Your Word says I should let You give me a new mind. When I live for You, doing the good things You have for me and standing apart from the sinfulness of the world around me, I show kindness by pointing others to You. Change my life the way You want, God. Amen.

....

How has God helped you so far
to stand apart from sinfulness?

PAYBACK

When someone does something bad to you, do not pay him back with something bad. Try to do what all men know is right and good. As much as you can, live in peace with all men. Christian brothers, never pay back someone for the bad he has done to you. Let the anger of God take care of the other person. The Holy Writings say, "I will pay back to them what they should get, says the Lord." "If the one who hates you is hungry, feed him. If he is thirsty, give him water. If you do that, you will be making him more ashamed of himself." Do not let sin have power over you. Let good have power over sin!

ROMANS 12:17–21

Dear God, when somebody is mean to me or a friend or family member, sometimes my first reaction is to want to get even. I want the mean person to hurt the way they hurt someone else. But Your Word has specific instructions for situations like this in Romans 12. Please help me to follow Your instructions, even when doing so is super hard. Amen.

Have you ever stepped back from wanting revenge and then seen God work out justice?

GOD KNOWS

O Lord, You have looked through me and have known me.
You know when I sit down and when I get up. You understand
my thoughts from far away. You look over my path and my lying
down. You know all my ways very well. Even before I speak
a word, O Lord, You know it all. You have closed me in from
behind and in front. And You have laid Your hand upon me.
All You know is too great for me. It is too much for me
to understand. Where can I go from Your Spirit?
Or where can I run away from where You are?

PSALM 139:1–7

Dear God, You are always watching every person and know everything they think, say, and do. I guess some people might be a little creeped out by that, but they must not know how loving and awesome You are! Help me to show others how good You are to know us and watch us and care for us so well. You are with us to help and guide us if we let You. Amen.

What is most comforting to you in knowing
that God is always watching you?

BE A DOER

Obey the Word of God. If you hear only and do not act, you are
only fooling yourself. Anyone who hears the Word of God and
does not obey is like a man looking at his face in a mirror.
After he sees himself and goes away, he forgets what he looks
like. But the one who keeps looking into God's perfect
Law and does not forget it will do what it says and
be happy as he does it. God's Word makes men free.

JAMES 1:22–25

Dear God, please help me never just to read and listen to Your Word without doing what it says. Reading and listening and then acting out Your Word is how I constantly learn and grow in Your kindness and share it with others. I'm just a kid, but I can start focusing on obedience to Your Word now and continue it all of my life. Please help me. Amen.

How can you tell when someone only
hears God's Word but doesn't do it?

POWERFUL TONGUES

*We all make many mistakes. If anyone does not make a mistake
with his tongue by saying the wrong things, he is a perfect man.
It shows he is able to make his body do what he wants it to do.
We make a horse go wherever we want it to go by a small bit
in its mouth. We turn its whole body by this. Sailing ships are
driven by strong winds. But a small rudder turns a large
ship whatever way the man at the wheel wants the
ship to go. The tongue is also a small part of
the body, but it can speak big things.*

JAMES 3:2–5

Dear God, if I want to be kind in what I say to others,
I need to remember all the time how powerful Your
Word says my tongue is. I'm thankful You know how
easy it is to make mistakes with my words, but please
help me to be careful what I say to others and to apologize when I mess up. Thank You! Amen.

What words have hurt you badly?
How have you hurt others with words?

POWERFUL PRAYER

The prayer from the heart of a man right with God has much power. Elijah was a man as we are. He prayed that it might not rain. It did not rain on the earth for three and one-half years. Then he prayed again that it would rain. It rained much and the fields of the earth gave fruit.

JAMES 5:16–18

Dear God, some people in our world think that praying to You means nothing and does nothing, but I know that's not true. Help me never to stop praying to You for the littlest of things and the biggest of things, in my life and in the lives of the family and friends I love and in the entire world of people around me. You care about every single thing, and You listen to and act on our prayers. I thank You and praise You! Amen.

How have you seen God answer both
little prayers and big prayers?

BIGGER, BETTER WAYS

"For My thoughts are not your thoughts, and My ways are
not your ways," says the Lord. "For as the heavens are higher
than the earth, so are My ways higher than your
ways, and My thoughts than your thoughts."

ISAIAH 55:8–9

Dear God, as I pray for myself and others, I need to remember that Your Word says Your ways are much, much bigger and better than mine. How You answer prayer is sometimes a whole lot different than what I or anyone expects. And sometimes we don't see answers to prayer for a very long time. Please strengthen my faith during the times it would be easy to wimp out in my belief—like when I'm waiting on You or confused by You. I want to help others believe in the power of prayer and in the goodness of Your ways even when I don't always understand them. Amen.

....

Has there been a time when God totally
shocked you with the unexpected way He
answered prayer? What happened?

AROUND YOUR NECK AND ON YOUR HEART

*Do not let kindness and truth leave you. Tie them around your
neck. Write them upon your heart. So you will find favor
and good understanding in the eyes of God and man.
Trust in the Lord with all your heart, and do not trust in
your own understanding. Agree with Him in all
your ways, and He will make your paths straight.*

PROVERBS 3:3–6

Dear God, Your Word says You want me to keep kindness tied around my neck? That sounds a little weird at first, but then I get it. It's just a way to say You want kindness close to me. Along with truth, kindness should be so ingrained in me it's as if it is written on my heart. I like how kindness and truth go together like peanut butter and jelly in this scripture. When I keep Your kindness and truth close to me, constantly focusing on them in my life and trusting You, You will keep me on the best path that leads closer and closer to perfect forever with You. Amen.

....

How do you see God keeping your paths straight when
you trust Him and let Him lead?

EVERY GOOD THING

*Whatever is good and perfect comes to us from God. He is the
One Who made all light. He does not change. No shadow is
made by His turning. He gave us our new lives through the
truth of His Word only because He wanted to.
We are the first children in His family.*

JAMES 1:17–18

Dear God, please remind me all the time that everything good comes from You and everything I have is Yours. Yes, my parents work to provide me with things, but their ability to work comes from You! Nobody comes into this world with anything and no one leaves with anything (1 Timothy 6:7). So please help me use all the time I'm given on this earth to share with kindness the good gifts that come from You, God. Thank You! Amen.

. . . .

What good things in your life do you find it hardest to be generous with? How can you let God help you?

NEVER ALONE

"Be strong and have strength of heart. Do not be afraid or shake with fear because of them. For the Lord your God is the One Who goes with you. He will be faithful to you. He will not leave you alone."

DEUTERONOMY 31:6

Dear God, only You can absolutely promise never to leave anyone alone. I often want to promise a friend or family member that I will always be there for them, but the truth is, I can't always keep that promise. I will try my best to be a good and loyal friend and loved one, but a lot of things in life are out of my control. But You, God, are always faithful and will never leave any of us. Remind me of that truth every day, and help me to remind others. Amen.

Have you experienced a time when someone let you down but you realized God was with you anyway?

EVEN IF

You are being kept by the power of God because you put your trust in Him and you will be saved from the punishment of sin at the end of the world. With this hope you can be happy even if you need to have sorrow and all kinds of tests for awhile. These tests have come to prove your faith and to show that it is good. Gold, which can be destroyed, is tested by fire. Your faith is worth much more than gold and it must be tested also.

1 Peter 1:5–7

Dear God, the sad and hard times in life never seem like they can be described as good. At the time, they just seem awful. But this scripture makes me think about them differently. Anyone who trusts You will be saved, and we have an awesome hope because of that—hope that can make us happy even while we go through hard things. Please help me to remember that sorrow and tests aren't necessarily totally bad. Sometimes they are a kindness from You to prove my faith. Help me to understand and share this truth with others. Amen.

What tests of your faith have you gone through?

GRATEFUL FOR ANY GIFT

Always give thanks for all things to God the Father in the name of our Lord Jesus Christ.

EPHESIANS 5:20

Dear God, sometimes on my birthday or at Christmas, I get gifts that really aren't my favorite or what I was hoping for. Sometimes it's hard to know what to say or do when I open a present that's disappointing. I need Your help to keep a better attitude. Help me to have a grateful heart and show kindness and appreciation to the person who has given the gift, no matter what it is. People and relationships are always more important than things. Please help me always to remember that. Amen.

Have you ever received a gift you
didn't like? How did you react?

SHARP FRIENDS

Iron is made sharp with iron,
and one man is made sharp by a friend.

PROVERBS 27:17

Dear God, in my friendships with other Christians, please help us encourage each other to constantly learn and grow, especially in our relationship with You! I want to challenge my friends in good ways, and I want them to do the same for me. Help us to have a good influence on others, and keep bad influences away from us. Help us to remind each other to spend time with You in Your Word, in prayer, and at church. We want to know You more, God, and we want to live for You—as kids now and as grown-ups later! Amen.

....

Which friends help you to be a better person?
How do you do the same for them?

PET PEEVES

Live and work without pride. Be gentle and kind.
Do not be hard on others. Let love keep you from doing
that. Work hard to live together as one by the help
of the Holy Spirit. Then there will be peace.

EPHESIANS 4:2–3

Dear God, sometimes annoying little things can drive me big-time crazy! Those are my pet peeves. Some kids at school have little habits that get on my nerves, and my siblings and parents do too. I need Your help, God, to be kind when I'm irritated by these little things. Sometimes the frustration builds up and just wants to explode! But You can help me stop the eruption. Help me to remember that I probably also do certain things that annoy others, so I need to have patience with everyone. Amen.

What are your pet peeves?

COVERED WITH HIS WINGS

He who lives in the safe place of the Most High will be in the shadow of the All-powerful. I will say to the Lord, "You are my safe and strong place, my God, in Whom I trust." For it is He Who takes you away from the trap, and from the killing sickness. He will cover you with His wings. And under His wings you will be safe. He is faithful like a safe-covering and a strong wall. You will not be afraid of trouble at night, or of the arrow that flies by day. You will not be afraid of the sickness that walks in darkness, or of the trouble that destroys at noon.

PSALM 91:1–6

Dear God, a lot of things in life can seem scary, and I know my friends and siblings feel scared sometimes too. Please remind me to trust in Your all-powerful care and protection when I'm scared. And help me to share kindness by telling others about Your protection too. You are our safe place. Amen.

....

When have you seen God's protection
in your life or a friend's life?

STEPPING IN OR STEPPING BACK

Everyone must do his own work.

GALATIANS 6:5

Dear God, a classmate said to me once that I was mean if I didn't let her copy my homework. But I don't think I was being mean at all. I think I was being kind to let her take responsibility for her own work and learn about consequences if she didn't do it herself. Please give me wisdom about this type of thing my whole life. Sometimes it's definitely kind to do something for another person, but sometimes it's even kinder to let others do something themselves so they can learn from the experience. I need You to show me when to step in for someone and when to step back and let them handle the situation. Thank You for Your help! Amen.

Have you ever stepped in to help a friend when your help was much needed? Have you ever stepped back when you knew a friend needed to do something on their own?

TIME WISE

Be wise in the way you live around those who are
not Christians. Make good use of your time.

COLOSSIANS 4:5

Dear God, managing time well can seem like a grown-up thing, but help me to realize how important time management is for me even now. I won't do much good with my life if I'm constantly wasting time. But if I use time wisely, I'll be able to do more, learn more, and share more kindness with others. In all of that, I want to give praise and glory to You. You give me the ability to do any good thing with my time. Thank You! Amen.

Do you feel like you manage your time well,
or could you improve your time management?

IN HIS IMAGE

Then God said, "Let Us make man like Us and let him be head over the fish of the sea, and over the birds of the air, and over the cattle, and over all the earth, and over every thing that moves on the ground." And God made man in His own likeness. In the likeness of God He made him. He made both male and female.

GENESIS 1:26–27

Dear God, I seem to hear a lot these days about people trying to figure out their identity. To me, it doesn't seem as complicated as others make it sound. Your Word is clear in the first book, Genesis, that You made us in Your likeness. You've made boys and girls to grow up into men and women, and You've given us the Bible to guide us in how to live and love like You. Help me to kindly and lovingly share that simple, powerful truth with others. And please help me to follow You forever. Amen.

．．．

How do you picture God, knowing that you are made
in His likeness, and how does that
image of Him inspire you?

TRUST IN HIM

You have never seen Him but you love Him. You cannot see Him now but you are putting your trust in Him. And you have joy so great that words cannot tell about it. You will get what your faith is looking for, which is to be saved from the punishment of sin.

1 PETER 1:8–9

Dear God, sometimes kids who don't believe in You are mean to me about my faith in You. When that happens, help me to remember this scripture and choose kindness toward them anyway. I do love You even though I don't see You the same as I see people here with me. I see You in other ways as I put my trust in You again and again, and You fill me with joy so big I can't even fully explain it. Please keep doing that! I know You are the one and only Savior from sin. Help me to keep choosing kindness and love. I want to help point others to You, no matter what. Amen.

Have you ever faced ridicule because of
your faith but chose kindness anyway?

ABOVE AND BEYOND

Then Peter came to Jesus and said, "Lord, how many times may my brother sin against me and I forgive him, up to seven times?" Jesus said to him, "I tell you, not seven times but seventy times seven!"

MATTHEW 18:21–22

Dear God, when I'm angry with someone who has done something mean to me, it sure is hard to be kind in return. But the first step in showing kindness in those cases is being able to forgive. Your Word says I should go above and beyond in forgiving others, like not just seven times but seventy times seven. I definitely need Your help to offer forgiveness to those who keep sinning against me, God. You will have to be working within me, for sure, to help me do the forgiving—again and again and again. Thank You! Amen.

Have you experienced a time when God worked in you to forgive even though you didn't feel like offering forgiveness at first?

A BEAUTIFUL LIFE

We are allowed to do anything, but not everything is good for us to do. We are allowed to do anything, but not all things help us grow strong as Christians. Do not work only for your own good. Think of what you can do for others.

1 CORINTHIANS 10:23–24

Dear God, this scripture tells me that my life is not supposed to be lived only for myself and my own good. No, You want me to live my life thinking of what I can do for others. Then I end up with a lifetime of choosing kindness and sharing it with people around me. That sounds like a truly beautiful life, and that is the kind of life I want with Your powerful help! Please help me to grow strong as a Christian. Amen.

In what way have you seen God helping you grow strong as a Christian?

DON'T TRY TO HIDE

*I told my sin to You. I did not hide my wrong-doing. I said, "I will tell my sins to the Lord."
And You forgave the guilt of my sin.*

PSALM 32:5

Dear God, I can't very well choose kindness toward others if I have stuff going on in my own head and heart and actions that I know are wrong. Help me never try to hide my mistakes and sins from You, God. You see them anyway, and You want me to admit them to You and ask Your forgiveness. Thank You for giving it so quickly and generously! When my heart and mind are right with You, I can focus on the kind things You want me to do for others. Help to me share this truth with others too. Amen.

Have you experienced a time when you were holding on to sin and the sin was holding you back from the good things God wanted you to do?

ROCK OR SAND?

"Whoever hears these words of Mine and does them, will be like a wise man who built his house on rock. The rain came down. The water came up. The wind blew and hit the house. The house did not fall because it was built on rock. Whoever hears these words of Mine and does not do them, will be like a foolish man who built his house on sand. The rain came down. The water came up. The wind blew and hit the house. The house fell and broke apart."

MATTHEW 7:24–27

Dear God, I like learning from this parable about the houses built on rock and sand. Right now I'm thinking I can't share kindness with others if my own life isn't strong. And real strength for life comes from following You and Your Word. Help me to build on You, God my rock, not on crumbling sand. Amen.

....

What does it look like for someone's life to break apart because it isn't built on God's ways? What does it look like for someone's life to stand strong because it is built on God's ways?

BIG FANS

The one who says he belongs to Christ should
live the same kind of life Christ lived.

1 JOHN 2:6

Dear Jesus, sometimes I see other kids who are totally obsessed with famous athletes, singers, and movie stars. I'm a big fan of certain celebrities too, and I understand how easy it is to go over the top in our admiration of famous individuals. Please give me wisdom in this area, and help me to kindly share that wisdom with my friends and classmates. My main role model should always be You! I know it's okay to be inspired by others, but I need to remember that the only perfect human was You. Anyone else can easily let me down. Help me to be realistic in the way I view the people I look up to. Help me to constantly look higher than any human on earth, all the way up to You, as my inspiration and hope! Amen.

....

Have you experienced a time
when a role model let you down?

MONEY, MONEY, MONEY

The love of money is the beginning of all kinds of sin. Some people have turned from the faith because of their love for money. They have made much pain for themselves because of this.

1 TIMOTHY 6:10

Dear God, it's fun to think about having a good job that makes plenty of money someday. But Your Word says that should not be my goal. My goal should be to serve You and serve others. If I do make money now or far off in the future, please help me to remember it all comes from You and to do the good things You want me to do with it. Help me never to love money, but only to use it in ways that please You and share Your love and kindness with others. Amen.

How can you use money in ways that are wise
and pleasing to God even now as a kid?

KEEP ON PRAYING

*Jesus told them a picture-story to show that men
should always pray and not give up.*

LUKE 18:1

Dear God, I have friends and loved ones who don't know You as their Savior. I keep praying for them, but nothing seems to change. Help me to keep on loving them. Help me to remember the kindest thing I can do for them is to never give up praying for them. Give me the right words and actions to encourage them and point them to You. Use others in their lives too—people who know You as Savior and also can point them to You. Please soften their hearts to hear and accept Your truth. Amen.

Who are the people in your life you are praying
for to ask Jesus to be their Savior?

THE LIGHT OF THE WORLD

"You are the light of the world. You cannot hide a city that is on a mountain. Men do not light a lamp and put it under a basket. They put it on a table so it gives light to all in the house. Let your light shine in front of men. Then they will see the good things you do and will honor your Father Who is in heaven."

MATTHEW 5:14–16

Dear God, I like that Your Word calls me the light of the world. That sounds like a big deal, and it really is! The kindest thing I can do for others is shine light that leads them to You. I want them to see the good things in my life and know that every single one of them comes from You. Please help me to shine brightly to bring You glory, God. Amen.

....

What are specific ways you shine your light for Jesus?

DON'T PLAY FAVORITES

My Christian brothers, our Lord Jesus Christ is the Lord of shining-greatness. Since your trust is in Him, do not look on one person as more important than another. What if a man comes into your church wearing a gold ring and good clothes? And at the same time a poor man comes wearing old clothes. What if you show respect to the man in good clothes and say, "Come and sit in this good place"? But if you say to the poor man, "Stand up over there," or "Sit on the floor by my feet," are you not thinking that one is more important than the other? This kind of thinking is sinful.

JAMES 2:1–4

Dear God, Your Word clearly teaches that we should not look at one person as more important than another. We are all precious and loved by You! Help me to treat others equally, like You do! Amen.

....

Have you experienced a situation where someone played favorites? How did that make you feel?

MAKE THE BEST OF IT

The mind of a man plans his way,
but the Lord shows him what to do.

PROVERBS 16:9

Dear God, I sure feel disappointed when plans get ruined because of stuff I didn't expect—like my sister getting sick or my dad's car breaking down. In those times it's easy to whine and complain and be rude because I'm upset things didn't go my way. Help me choose not to do that. Help me to make the best of canceled plans with a good attitude and to be kind to everyone affected by the change. Help me to know You are working in the details in ways I don't even understand. We plan our ways, but You show us what to do, God, and You are always good and trustworthy. Amen.

What has been your most frustrating experience of canceled plans? How did you respond?

ALL I NEED

I have learned to be happy with whatever I have. I know how to get along with little and how to live when I have much. I have learned the secret of being happy at all times. If I am full of food and have all I need, I am happy. If I am hungry and need more, I am happy. I can do all things because Christ gives me the strength.

PHILIPPIANS 4:11–13

Dear God, it's easy to look around and compare my stuff and my grades and my opportunities and my friends with what others have in their lives. Help me not to do that. Help me to focus on doing my best with what You've given me—the talents, abilities, family, friends, and possessions. I want to be content with whatever You have decided to bless me with. You are always good and right and give just what I need! Amen.

In what ways are you most tempted to compare your life with others' lives?

TRUST ALONE

*Men become right with God by putting their trust in Jesus
Christ. God will accept men if they come this way. All men are
the same to God. For all men have sinned and have missed the
shining-greatness of God. Anyone can be made right with God
by the free gift of His loving-favor. It is Jesus Christ Who bought
them with His blood and made them free from their sins.*

ROMANS 3:22–24

Dear God, sometimes I hear people talking and acting
like the good stuff we do is what gets us to heaven.
But Your Word says salvation is all about putting our
trust in Jesus alone. No one could ever do enough
good stuff to match Your shining-greatness! So You
gave Your Son to take away our sin. I feel so much
freedom knowing that I don't have to work constantly
to get into heaven. You already have a place for me
there because I believe in Jesus Christ as my one and
only Savior. Help me to share this awesome truth with
others! Amen.

In what ways do you see people working hard to get
into heaven without truly trusting Jesus?

HELP TO OBEY

God is helping you obey Him. God is doing what He wants done in you. Be glad you can do the things you should be doing. Do all things without arguing and talking about how you wish you did not have to do them.

PHILIPPIANS 2:13–14

Dear God, trusting in You as my Savior motivates me to want to do good things for You. I want to serve You and help others know about You! Please don't ever stop helping me obey. I want to do anything You ask with no complaining. That includes listening to my parents and other leaders and teachers in my life and doing what they ask with no arguing or complaining. Having a good attitude is really hard sometimes, God, but I know with Your help, I can do it. And when I mess up, I can say I'm sorry and keep trying to do better. Amen.

When is it hardest for you to obey
and keep a good attitude?

THE REAL DEAL

Because we are telling the truth, we want men's hearts to listen to us. God knows our desires. If the Good News we preach is hidden, it is hidden to those who are lost in sin. The eyes of those who do not believe are made blind by Satan who is the god of this world. He does not want the light of the Good News to shine in their hearts. This Good News shines as the shining-greatness of Christ. Christ is as God is. We do not preach about ourselves. We preach Christ Jesus the Lord.

2 Corinthians 4:2–5

Dear God, help me to encourage others when we hear people make fun of being a Christian. Our enemy the devil has no reason to make fun of religions that don't mean anything. The fact that Christianity is laughed at and fought against gives encouragement that it is the real deal! Help me to keep living my life for You and sharing the Good News of Your love and saving grace. Amen.

....

Has anyone ever made fun of you for your faith in Jesus?

EXTRA-SPECIAL PEACE

"Peace I leave with you. My peace I give to you.
I do not give peace to you as the world gives.
Do not let your hearts be troubled or afraid."

JOHN 14:27

Dear Jesus, please give me Your peace. I can't do anything well or be very kind to anyone if I'm always feeling stressed and anxious. A lot of things in life make me feel troubled and afraid, but in Your Word You tell me not to be either of those. I want to listen to You and obey You, Jesus! Help me to take big, deep breaths and focus on Your power and love when I'm feeling troubled or afraid. Fill me with Your extra-special peace and refill me again and again as I live for You and share kindness with others. Amen.

....

What does it feel like to be filled with
the kind of peace Jesus gives?

SO MUCH MORE

God is able to do much more than we ask or think through His
power working in us. May we see His shining-greatness in the
church. May all people in all time honor Christ Jesus. Let it be so.

EPHESIANS 3:20–21

Dear God, I love this scripture and I need to remember it more often. I want to focus on it every single time I pray. Sometimes I worry that maybe You can't do what I'm asking for. And then it hits me that no matter what I'm asking for in prayer, You are able to do so much more than anything I ask or think. Your power is amazing, and I want to see it working through all Your people. Help me to keep trusting in You more and more, God! Amen.

....

Have you ever prayed for something and then God answered in a much bigger way than you expected?

LINE TIME

I wait for the Lord. My soul waits
and I hope in His Word.

PSALM 130:5

Dear God, I feel like I spend a whole lot of time waiting in lines—at school, at the grocery store, at the doctor's office. Waiting can seem like such a waste of time! Help me to make good use of my time in lines. I can smile and be friendly to the people waiting with me. I can help my mom load groceries to be scanned. I can chat with my dad. I can encourage my classmates. And always I can pray. Please help me to think of waiting time positively and make the best of it. Amen.

What is your least favorite place to wait in line
and why? What is your favorite place
to wait in line and why?

EVEN IN LITTLE THINGS

*He that is faithful with little things is faithful with big
things also. He that is not honest with little
things is not honest with big things.*

LUKE 16:10

Dear God, please help me to be faithful even in little things. Help me to be responsible with my stuff and to clean up the messes and clutter I make around the house, in my room, at my activities, at friends' houses, and when I'm working at school. Help me to clean up after myself without being asked and to care about the ways my stuff can affect others. I want to be kind and respectful of the people I share space with and do life with. Amen.

Are you a neat freak or on the messy side?
In what ways do you need to improve?

FAR AWAY

Turn away from the sinful things young people want to do.
Go after what is right. Have a desire for faith and love and
peace. Do this with those who pray to God from a clean heart.
Let me say it again. Have nothing to do with foolish talk
and those who want to argue. It can only lead to trouble.

2 TIMOTHY 2:22–23

Dear God, please help me to turn far away from things
You say are wrong and from people who try to get me
into trouble. If they won't listen and continue to try
to get me in trouble, I know it's okay to have nothing
to do with those people anymore. Choosing kindness
never means joining in with sin. Please help me to be
strong and brave about turning away from sin. Amen.

....

What wrong things are hardest
for you to turn away from?

THE BEST REST

*"Come to Me, all of you who work and have heavy loads.
I will give you rest. Follow My teachings and learn from
Me. I am gentle and do not have pride. You will have rest
for your souls. For My way of carrying a load
is easy and My load is not heavy."*

MATTHEW 11:28–30

Dear God, sometimes I don't want to slow down or miss out on fun things, so I don't want to rest. Help me to realize that's not smart. I need good rest to be able to do what You have planned for me and to show kindness along the way. Help me to follow and learn from You and get real rest, because working for You is never too hard or too tiring. Amen.

Do you ever feel a fear of missing out on
the things going on around you? Why?

LEARNING FROM DIFFERENCES

*Both of us need help. I can help make your faith strong
and you can do the same for me. We need each other.*

ROMANS 1:12

Dear God, I know a lot of different kids at church and from my activities who do all different types of school. There's public school, private school, online school, homeschool, even unschooling. As I get to know new friends, help me to reach out to kids who do school differently than me. It would be easy for everyone to just hang out with people similar to them. But I want to get to know others who are different from me too. We can learn so much from each other. We are all different and are all equally loved by You! We all need each other too. Help us to make each other strong in our faith in You! Amen.

....

What about school do you wish
you could do differently?

ALL THE MORE

Sin spread when the Law was given. But where sin spread,
God's loving-favor spread all the more. Sin had power that
ended in death. Now, God's loving-favor has power to
make men right with Himself. It gives life that lasts
forever. Our Lord Jesus Christ did this for us.

ROMANS 5:20–21

Dear God, sometimes I just don't feel like being kind to anyone, or I feel like I want to but just can't because all my kindness seems used up. In those times, help me remember Your loving-favor. When sin spread, Your grace and kindness spread all the more. I can't ever measure up to Your great love, but I want to keep trying to be more like You! You give such incredible kindness, and then You give and give and give some more! You spread it all over like the best kind of frosting spread on the biggest cake ever! Please keep filling me up with You, God, so that I can keep sharing kindness with others. Amen.

What makes you feel tired of spreading kindness?
How does God help you rest and recharge
so you can spread some more?

BEYOND UNDERSTANDING

*I pray that Christ may live in your hearts by faith. I pray that
you will be filled with love. I pray that you will be able to
understand how wide and how long and how high and how
deep His love is. I pray that you will know the love of Christ.
His love goes beyond anything we can understand.
I pray that you will be filled with God Himself.*

EPHESIANS 3:17–19

Dear God, I like this kind and loving prayer from Paul,
the author of the Bible's book of Ephesians. I want
to remember to pray it regularly for myself and for
my family and friends. We can never fully understand
Your great love for us, but please help us to focus on
trying. Fill us up to the very top and then let it overflow from us to others. Amen.

· ·

If you tried to draw a picture of God's super-huge
love for you, what would it look like?

164

BE CAREFUL

When you are around people who do not know God, be careful
how you act. Even if they talk against you as wrong-doers,
in the end they will give thanks to God for your
good works when Christ comes again.

1 PETER 2:12

Dear God, help me to remember that the way I live my life matters to those who don't know You. If I say I love and follow You and I know that unbelievers are watching my actions, I consistently need to be doing my best to make sure what I say matches up with what I do. Even if others talk negatively about me, it won't matter if what they say isn't true. If I keep being faithful to You, in the end they can give thanks to You for the good things they saw in me. I'm not totally sure how this works, God, but I trust You and want to obey You! Amen.

Has anyone ever said something bad but untrue about you? How did you respond?

WEAK = STRONG

He answered me, "I am all you need. I give you My loving-favor.
My power works best in weak people." I am happy to be
weak and have troubles so I can have Christ's
power in me. I receive joy when I am weak.

2 CORINTHIANS 12:9–10

Dear God, sometimes I feel like I am so worn out that I can't possibly share kindness with anyone. In those times, please remind me of this scripture. You say Your power works best in my weakness. In my tired, struggling moments, help me to be filled with joy and with Your amazing strength. I want to be reenergized by it and then continue to spread Your kindness and love. Thank You! Amen.

....

What makes you feel weakest? How has God
strengthened you in moments of weakness?

KINDNESS FOR THE UNKIND

"Love those who hate you. (*Respect and give thanks for those who say bad things to you. Do good to those who hate you.) Pray for those who do bad things to you and who make it hard for you."

<small>MATTHEW 5:44</small>

Dear God, being kind to someone who never seems to give any kindness back to me or others can be really hard. But please help me not to give up. I don't know what You might be doing behind the scenes in a person's life, and my kind actions might be helping them see Your love for them. Maybe they were never taught kindness by anyone. Help me be the one who teaches them. Sometimes the people who don't seem to know how to show kindness are the ones who need kindness the most. Amen.

Have you ever seen kindness change the heart and actions of someone who was being mean?

BRAG ABOUT GOD

*Christ bought us with His blood and made us free from our sins.
It is as the Holy Writings say, "If anyone is going to be
proud of anything, he should be proud of the Lord."*

1 CORINTHIANS 1:30–31

Dear God, thank You for the times I am doing great at school and in my activities. I'm grateful for the talents and abilities You've given me! When things are going well for me, please help me to keep a good attitude about them. I want to be humble like Your Word says to be. I want to remember that everything good comes from You. I don't want to be someone who brags in annoying ways. Help me only ever to brag about how awesome You are, in ways that make others want to know You and Your great love. Amen.

How do you feel when you hear
others bragging about themselves?

DEEP ROOTS

As you have put your trust in Christ Jesus the Lord to save you from the punishment of sin, now let Him lead you in every step. Have your roots planted deep in Christ. Grow in Him. Get your strength from Him. Let Him make you strong in the faith as you have been taught. Your life should be full of thanks to Him.

COLOSSIANS 2:6–7

Dear God, with this scripture as a goal for my life, I will be content and able to do all the good and kind things You ask me to do. Please lead me in every step. Help me to grow in You with roots like a tree, deeply planted in Your love and truth. Please be my strength at all times, and strengthen my faith in You. I thank You and praise You always! Amen.

....

What does your life look like if you have
your roots planted deep in Christ?

GENTLE WITH WORDS

A gentle answer turns away anger, but a sharp word causes anger. The tongue of the wise uses much learning in a good way, but the mouth of fools speaks in a foolish way.

PROVERBS 15:1–2

Dear God, when people speak rudely to me, please help me not to speak angrily back to them. Your Word says I need a gentle answer to turn away anger. Giving a gentle answer is super-duper hard sometimes, God! But I know You can help me with this. Help me to use my words in good ways that make You happy and to work things out with friends and family rather than creating more anger and fighting. I don't want to be a fool who can speak only in foolish ways. Amen.

How do you feel when you say mean words to someone? How do you feel when you use self-control and speak gently instead?

LOVING LISTENER

I love the Lord, because He hears my voice and my prayers.
I will call on Him as long as I live, because He
has turned His ear to me.

PSALM 116:1–2

Dear God, since I'm young, sometimes I feel like I can't do much to show kindness and help others, but then I realize sometimes the best kindness is just to listen. Many times, people just want to be able to share their hurt and know that someone cares enough to hear them and hug them and pray for them. Please help me never to forget how important listening can be. You are a good listener, Lord. You hear our voices and prayers and turn Your ear to us. Help me to make time to be a good listener to others like You are and to share with others that You are the very best listener. Amen.

How do you feel knowing that
God always listens to you?

EMBARRASSING MOMENTS

Let yourself be brought low before the Lord. Then He will lift you up and help you. Christian brothers, do not talk against anyone or speak bad things about each other.

JAMES 4:10–11

Dear God, help me to be kind when I see someone in an embarrassing situation. Give me wisdom to know what they need me to do—sometimes I might need to step in and help, while other times I might need to step back and do nothing so I don't call attention to the situation. If it seems like it might help, maybe I can share a similar embarrassing story to help the person feel better. I can also remind others that we all make silly mistakes and nothing changes Your great love for us! Amen.

What is the story of your most embarrassing moment?

LOOK BACK

*I will remember the things the Lord has done. Yes, I will
remember the powerful works of long ago. I will think of all
Your work, and keep in mind all the great things You have
done. O God, Your way is holy. What god is great like
our God? You are the God Who does great works.
You have shown Your power among the people.*

PSALM 77:11–14

Dear God, help me to look back a lot and remember
the ways You have helped me in the past and the great
things You have done for me. Help me to remember
what You have done for others too. The Bible records
many of Your great works, and people throughout his-
tory and today are still telling of Your help and power
and miracles. When family or friends are feeling discouraged, help me to remind them to look back, remember Your great works in their lives, and then trust
You all the more for the future.

....

What are your favorite memories of great things
God has done in your life?

YOUNG LEADERS

*In all things show them how to live by your life and by right
teaching. You should be wise in what you say. Then the one
who is against you will be ashamed and will not
be able to say anything bad about you.*

TITUS 2:7–8

Dear God, help me to know how to be a good and
kind leader. As I'm following You, I can always lead
others who might not believe in You yet or who have
just begun to believe in You. No matter what my age,
what matters is that I'm living my life the best I can
according to the teaching of Your Word. Bring others
to me whom You want me to lead, God, and help me
to know the kindness and love and wisdom You want
me to help teach them. Amen.

• •

In what ways have you been a leader for God already
in your life, or how do you hope to be one?

PRAYING GOD'S WILL

We are sure that if we ask anything that He wants us to have,
He will hear us. If we are sure He hears us when we ask,
we can be sure He will give us what we ask for.

1 JOHN 5:14–15

Dear God, please help me to remember to pray for Your will to be done. You know all things and You are love itself. Everything You do is good and right. When I pray, help me to remember that You see things from a much broader view than I do. Prayer should be less about asking You to do what I want and more about surrendering my heart and mind so You can shape them to be like Yours and to want what You want. Help me to share this truth with others too. Amen.

How can you focus your prayers to better
match your will with God's will?

ALL DAY LONG

My mouth will tell about how right and good You are and about Your saving acts all day long. For there are more than I can know. I will come in the strength of the Lord God. I will tell about how right and good You are, and You alone. O God, You have taught me from when I was young. And I still tell about Your great works. Even when I am old and my hair is turning white, O God, do not leave me alone. Let me tell about Your strength to all the people living now, and about Your power to all who are to come.

PSALM 71:15–18

Dear God, may this scripture be true of me for my whole life! I never want to stop sharing with others about how awesome You are! Starting now while I'm young until I'm old and gray, I want to share great kindness with others by telling all about You! Amen.

....

What are some simple ways you can tell others
about God's greatness every single day?

WHY SO SAD?

Why are you sad, O my soul? Why have you become
troubled within me? Hope in God, for I will
praise Him again, my help and my God.

PSALM 43:5

Dear God, please help me on those days when I just feel like being sad and negative for no good reason. Yes, we all face many hard things in life. I can admit them and talk about them with You. But please take the negative thoughts from me and help me to focus on all the reasons I have to be joyful because You are my hope and Savior. I know it's okay to feel sad, but I don't always have to stay stuck in sadness. Help me to deal with up-and-down emotions well and be able to choose kindness in the midst of them. Amen.

....

Do you notice you feel sadder at certain times than at others? How has God helped you in those times?

KINDNESS IN SUFFERING?

Dear friends, your faith is going to be tested as if it were going through fire. Do not be surprised at this. Be happy that you are able to share some of the suffering of Christ. When His shining-greatness is shown, you will be filled with much joy.

1 PETER 4:12–13

Dear God, Your Word tells us to be happy to share some of the suffering of Jesus Christ. I'm not sure exactly what that means, but please keep teaching me. I think it means we grow closer to You and understand You better when we share in sufferings like you endured so much to save us from sin. And I think it means when You make all things right someday, You will reward us in big ways for continuing to trust in You even while going through terrible things. Please keep me close and learning more about this subject from You, God. I love and trust You, no matter what. Amen.

....

What hard things have you suffered
but kept your faith through?

SAYING YOU'RE SORRY

Tell your sins to each other. And pray for
each other so you may be healed.

JAMES 5:16

Dear God, sometimes the kindest thing I can do is just be willing to admit my mistakes and say I'm sorry to others I have been unkind to. Help me to remember how important that is. These days too many people don't want to admit they've done something wrong and don't want to talk about their shortcomings. Admitting that we've made a mistake is never easy; that's for sure! But I want to be humble and apologize when I need to. I sure need Your help in this area, God. Thank You for giving it! Amen.

....

How do you feel when you apologize and work things out rather than just trying to ignore mistakes?

MESSY MEDIA

If then you have been raised with Christ, keep looking for the good things of heaven. This is where Christ is seated on the right side of God. Keep your minds thinking about things in heaven. Do not think about things on the earth.

COLOSSIANS 3:1–2

Dear God, there are so many different types of TV shows, movies, and music these days. The pressure to stay up to date on all of them can be overwhelming! Help me not to get caught up in all the trendy things to watch and listen to. I know some of it is so bad for me and so far away from what Your Word teaches. Help me to kindly keep myself away from media that makes You sad, God, and please help me to encourage others to do the same. Amen.

....

What are your favorite TV shows, movies, and music? Would God be pleased to watch or listen to them with you?

NEW EVERY MORNING

This I remember, and so I have hope. It is because of the Lord's loving-kindness that we are not destroyed for His loving-pity never ends. It is new every morning. He is so very faithful.
LAMENTATIONS 3:21–23

Dear God, if I know a friend or family member has turned away from You because they feel like they've messed up too much, help me to remind them how faithful and loving You are, no matter what they've done. Help me to remember this truth for myself too. Your grace and forgiveness are endless when we turn back to You. You give us fresh new kindness and never-ending love every morning. Thank You! Amen.

When you wake up each morning, how can you picture and focus on God's fresh loving-kindness toward you for that day?

NOTHING CAN KEEP US AWAY

For I know that nothing can keep us from the love of God.
Death cannot! Life cannot! Angels cannot! Leaders cannot!
Any other power cannot! Hard things now or in the future
cannot! The world above or the world below cannot! Any other
living thing cannot keep us away from the love of God
which is ours through Christ Jesus our Lord.
ROMANS 8:38–39

Dear God, thank You for this truth from Your Word, reminding us that absolutely *nothing* can keep us away from Your love. Help me to memorize this scripture and never forget it. And help me to kindly share it with others. Nobody loves like You do, God. You are our hope and Savior for right now and forever. Thank You! Amen.

In a difficult situation, how does your thinking change when you focus on the fact that nothing can keep you away from God's love?

LOSE THE LAZINESS

Go to the ant, O lazy person. Watch and think about her ways, and be wise. She has no leader, head or ruler, but she gets her food ready in the summer, and gathers her food at the right time. How long will you lie down, O lazy person? When will you rise up from your sleep? A little sleep, a little rest, a little folding of the hands to rest, and being poor will come upon you like a robber, and your need like a man ready to fight.

PROVERBS 6:6–11

Dear God, when I'm feeling bored, please help me to turn the boredom into kindness instead. Laziness and a bad attitude don't do anyone any good. When I feel like I have nothing to do, remind me there are always things I can do to help others and share kindness. Your Word talks a lot about not being lazy. Help me to work hard doing the good things You have planned for me, God. Thank You! Amen.

How do you balance getting good
rest with not being lazy?

FULL ARMOR

Put on all the things God gives you to fight with. . . . Wear a belt
of truth around your body. Wear a piece of iron over your chest
which is being right with God. Wear shoes on your feet which
are the Good News of peace. Most important of all, you need a
covering of faith in front of you. This is to put out the fire-arrows
of the devil. The covering for your head is that you have been
saved from the punishment of sin. Take the sword
of the Spirit which is the Word of God.

EPHESIANS 6:13–17

Dear God, I know my enemy the devil doesn't want me to choose kindness every day. He wants to attack me and stop me from showing Your love and truth to others. Please help me to fight him away every day! I need full body armor like Your Word describes. Help me to focus on putting it on each day so I can do the good and kind things You have planned for me without the devil defeating me! Amen.

How do you picture yourself wearing
the full armor of God?

FOREVER TREASURE

"Do not gather together for yourself riches of this earth. They will be eaten by bugs and become rusted. Men can break in and steal them. Gather together riches in heaven where they will not be eaten by bugs or become rusted. Men cannot break in and steal them."

MATTHEW 6:19–20

Dear God, help me to remember that choosing kindness here on earth doesn't always give me a quick reward. Sometimes I won't see any reward at all for choosing kindness. But Your Word says to store up "forever treasure" in heaven where nothing and no one can ruin it. I know You are watching me and keeping track of the good and kind things I do and stockpiling treasure for me in heaven. Even if no one else notices or appreciates kindness in me, I know You do, God, and that's what matters. Thank You! Amen.

....

Have you experienced a time when you chose kindness but felt like no one appreciated it but God?

EVERY DAY

Teach us to understand how many days we have.
Then we will have a heart of wisdom to give You.

PSALM 90:12

Dear God, only You know how many days each of us will live on this earth. Your Word says You have all our days numbered. Help me to live my days well. Help me to choose the kindness You teach in Your Word every day because it blesses me, blesses others, and, most importantly, blesses You! I want to be known as a person who loves and follows You and has Your kindness overflowing from me all the time. Amen.

What new things have you learned about choosing kindness from this book?

SCRIPTURE INDEX